Plan and launch your coaching business in 12 steps

Let's get focused

Stephanie A Thompson

Stephanie Thompson **Coaching**
Focused approaches for coaches

First Published in 2022 by Stephanie A Thompson

Book cover and graphics used within this book were created by Stephanie A Thompson using the free version of Canva.com

Further information about working with Stephanie can be found at the following website, or writing to the email mentioned above.

www.stephaniethompsoncoaching.com

Dedication

For Mum and Dad.
Thank you for showing me just what dedication and commitment can achieve. You are and continue to be awesome and an inspiration.

For Samantha, Alexandra,
Wayne, Luciana and Gwithian.
You light up my world and make everything worthwhile, always.

Content

Acknowledgments

Mum and Dad, I wouldn't be here if not for you meeting each other too many years ago to mention! I would not have the commitment or dedication without you showing me how important it is to work towards your dreams. Thank you for setting the standard. You are my pillars; I hope I make you proud.

A massive thank you to my two amazing daughters, Sam and Alex. You have always supported me in whatever I do, no matter what. I couldn't have done it without you. I think you are both awesome in totally different ways. You are my rocks.

Thank you to my fantastic group of friends who are there when I am celebrating and also there when times are tough. On the whole, fortunately, it's usually the former. You are always ready with a cuppa, a gin or fizz, a curry and your very sage and wise advice. Thank you Vivie, Meg, Chig, Deb 3Cs, Deb Sprinkles, Lorri, Emma, and Carole.

I would also like to give thanks to all the coaches I have worked with over the years, who have shared their extensive knowledge with me. It has been and continues to be, an honour to spend time in your energy. Thank you.

Finally, I would like to say thank you, thank you, thank you to my most amazing clients past, present, and future. You are all phenomenal. I love seeing your business grow and evolve as we work together. If you dream it, you can do it. And boy, do you do it …… it is an honour to work with you!

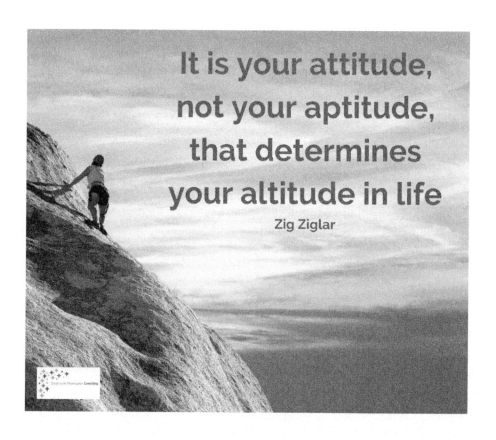

It is your attitude,
not your aptitude,
that determines
your altitude in life

Zig Ziglar

Introduction

I so remember when I first began as a coach. Although I had significant business knowledge, learned and experiential, I still felt like a rabbit in headlights in the beginning, until I began to see the pattern.

I don't want you to have to go through the overwhelm and frustration that I went through, which is why I founded the Get Focused Academy.

You can dip into different sections, depending on where you are in your business journey, or you can start at the beginning and work through each step.

What I will share is that, as my own online coaching business evolved and those magical patterns emerged, it all comes down to ten key steps. If you have your awesome coaching skills, but don't know where to start to set up your coaching business then this book is ideal and will share all the basics you need in place.

If you have any questions, please don't hesitate to contact me at stephanie@stephaniethompsoncoaching.com

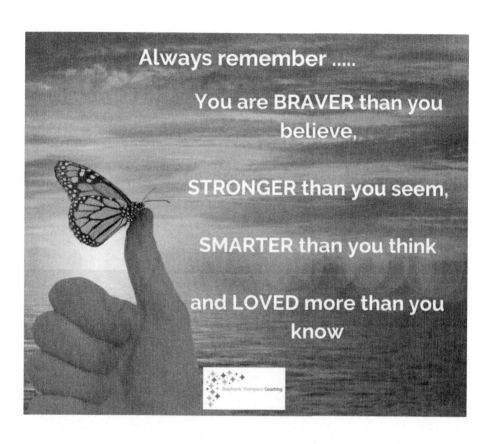

Always remember .....

You are BRAVER than you believe,

STRONGER than you seem,

SMARTER than you think

and LOVED more than you know

Chapter 1

Well hello and welcome

It wasn't until I watched a number of my old training videos that I realised I began them all with "well hello and welcome", so it seemed appropriate to start my first Chapter the same.

I am thrilled you have chosen to read this book and I can't tell you how excited I am to write it.

I will admit up front I absolutely adore business and I love to coach, so being a business empowerment coach is perfect for me. I am all about getting focused and this book is full of practical steps to get your coaching business established, launch your programme, get globally visible, attract clients and make a profit, alongside some tales of my adventures as a coach. I accept it is a massive promise but what I am going to be sharing with you is the exact same steps I took in my business, that resulted in my becoming an international coach, number one international best-selling author and an international radio host with my own show "Stephanie's Business Coaching Show" broadcasting into 47 different countries.

As I sit now writing and looking back on my coaching career it really didn't take all that long to get established. What it did take was FOCUS, determination and a good coach to guide me.

Having FOCUS is essential.

FOCUS on why you are doing what you are doing.

FOCUS on the focus.
- Foundations
- Opportunities
- Courage
- Understanding
- Shine

I bring a wide range of experience to this book – running 3 successful companies of my own, my parents were self-employed from when I was eleven, my ex-husband was also self-employed, I worked in a small-medium enterprise, as Chief Buyer, for 8 years, followed by being a manager in a number of departments at Rolls-Royce Aerospace including supplier development, apprenticeships and innovation, followed by consultancy work in companies such as JCB, Derby College and MTC.

Don't worry, it is not going to be a stodgy read, I hope you feel like I am sitting chatting with you over a coffee plus I have lots of stories to share too.

So where to start?

First things first, for this book to be of assistance then ideally you will already have your coaching skills either you have completed a training programme, or you held a training or coaching type role in your day job and are now transferring those skills across, or you are a whizz at your hobby and now want to share your passion with others.

Alternatively, you have been using your coaching skills working with family and friends, you get fantastic results and now it is time to get visible and be paid for your skills.

Rest assured your coaching is needed by so many people. Whatever your topic, someone needs it. It's time to take courage, get out there, and show those potential clients where to find you.

I have heard many times "I'm too old to start now". Rest assured this is not the case. You have really valuable life experiences that will help others grow and thrive. You've got this!!

So, if you are ready to walk towards your dreams, be the star you truly are, and live the life you deserve, then let's get started, focus and shine.

Chapter 2

Is your big why compelling enough?

Walt Disney said words to the effect of "If you can dream it, you can do it" and these are very, very powerful words.

The mind does not know the difference between imagination and reality.

Don't believe me?

Take a moment to sit back. Close your eyes and relax in your chair. Tilt your head slightly upwards and feel the sun shining on your face. Feel the warmth on your arms and legs. You can hear the rhythmic sound of the sea washing up against the shore. In your minds-eye, you can see the beautiful deep turquoise of the ocean and powder-soft white sand before you. You can hear the birds singing in the trees behind you and hear the breeze gently rustling the leaves. Take a few deep breaths and smell that clean sea air. And what else is that you can smell? In the not too far distance, you can smell the barbeque they are cooking for lunch. You imagine your hand reaching out to pick up a drink and you relax deep into your chair knowing that you don't have a care in the world.

Just take a few more deep breaths and really relax into it..

Now slowly bring yourself back to reality.

Are you back in the room?

Do you feel as though you have just had a lovely mini-break and replenished your soul?

This is how strong the mind is at conjuring up its own images and does not know the difference between imagination and reality.

Going back to my original question, after our little trip to the beach, "is your big why compelling enough"?

I am going to use "big why", but you could replace it with vision, goal, dream – they all lead to the same – your big why for doing what you do. Your reason for getting up in the morning. Your reason for choosing to work instead of watching TV, or pegging the washing out.

Or do you find yourself trying to grow your business in the last hour of the day; when all you want to do is crash out on the sofa? Because you've spent most of the day running around after others? Helping them out – to achieve their dreams and desires?

Using the example of our trip to the beach, just think, if you take that same concept and apply it to something much bigger in your life, very big – like your business, or an area of your life you want to improve.

We do not have to live with what life has dealt us. It is within our power to change things, to achieve great things!!!!

There are several distinct areas that I want to share with you about a compelling big why, (although we might digress along the way), I do want to talk with you about:

- o Traditional and energy vision boards. Energy Vision Boards are my favourite, I hope you like the idea of them as much as I like them when I share my stories with you.
- o How to make your vision really compelling.
- o Where to put your vision board – I love a bit of Feng Shui, don't you? I am no expert, but I will be sharing a couple of things that I do which has made a huge difference to my rapidly expanding business
- o How to plan to achieve your big why.
- o Why it is important to celebrate your big why.

Let me begin by asking ... do you have a traditional vision board? You know - the one with a posh car, a 5-star holiday, luxury spa day, maybe a posh watch or jewellery - that sort of thing. I remember those days. I used to create one every year and it would be pinned to the side of my fridge for the whole year. But by mid-February it just became part of the décor and I never really took any notice of it. Occasionally I would think – "Yes I must invite the family for dinner", prompted by one of the pictures I was looking at whilst on the phone, but that was about it!

For all my commitment when I created the vision board, it never really inspired me. I never really got behind the reasoning for vision board, although I did enjoy the creativity of making one. It reminded me of school days with lots of paper and scissors and glue, bits of magazine stuck to the carpet. Do you remember those activities?

Then, a few years ago, I was introduced to Energy Vision Boards. Boy did that open my eyes and now I use this technique to create one every 6 months. In fact, several of my friends love this technique so much we all get together and spend the day laughing and chatting and creating our energy vision boards. There are piles of magazines and scissors, glue and stickers all over my kitchen table. It takes us nearly 20 minutes to clear the table so we can have lunch! Then we have the joy of starting all over again. It is a fabulous bonding time and all achieved whilst we are in flow.

"Stephanie, how do you get in flow?" I hear you ask. I have trained to be a mentor, which is an eighteen-month personal journey, and use the Energy Alignment Method (EAM), created by Yvette Taylor, to help get myself and others into flow. I'll talk about it a bit more, later on in the book and even share some exercises too. But let's get back to creating energy vision boards …

After I have checked with each lady present there is no resistance and she is fully in flow I lead the group through a guided relaxing meditation. The meditation inspires each individual's energy and the next step is to allow their energy to choose what goes on their vision board and where it should be placed. Often, in the beginning, there is no comprehension as to why words or pictures are included on their board. However, what I can tell you is soooo so much has come true over the years you would not believe! Here is an example of what I experienced as a result of my first vision board …

One picture I was guided to include on my first Energy Vision Board, was of a lady standing on some steps of a brownstone house in New York. I had absolutely no plans of going to New York at that time. Within eight months I was travelling from San Diego home to the UK and unexpectedly had a twelve-hour delay at JFK Airport, near New York. I had met a lovely lady, Tricia, at the conference in San Diego, who had gone home the day earlier. In an exchange of texts whilst checking she was home safe, I shared I had the delay she said "come and spend the day with me" so that is exactly what I did.

For the first time ever, I used the New York subway. At one point I was in the right station on the wrong platform getting on the wrong train, but hey ho, these things happen. Tricia was a gem and kept sending me messages get off at this stop, change to this platform, get on this train etc.

I eventually managed to get myself to where I was meeting Tricia. Phew!!!! It was so lovely to see her smiling face after getting a little lost in the subway.

I walked out into the sunshine, looking straight onto the brownstone houses of Brooklyn!!!! You could have knocked me down with a feather! I had been so busy trying to make sure I was on the correct trains I had not registered I was heading to Brooklyn, NOR did I realise that Brooklyn is home of the brownstone houses. I do now!

I had a wonderful day in her company walking across the Brooklyn Bridge, taking lots of photos, seeing the Statue of Liberty from her apartment rooftop garden, having a fabulous lunch and of course, during the day I just had to have some photos taken of me being in the exact same pose as the lady in the picture on my Energy Vision Board. It was a wonderful experience and one I shall treasure! Such a shame I can't show you the photos here. However, if you ever decide to join one of my Energy Vision Board events you will certainly get to see them.

Oh dear, now I am in flow with telling you about energy vision boards I am going to have to share another story with you …

The picture on my board was of a beach. Blue skies, large sandy dunes covered in tall grass blowing in the wind, with a little picket-type fence following the walkway down to the sea. Got the picture? I had absolutely no idea where it was, or what it was doing on my board.

Well … I travelled to the Netherlands for a conference, arriving late at night in the dark. I booked into my hotel and had a very very early start. It wasn't until about 3pm in the afternoon that I managed to get outside for a breath of fresh air. I walked out of the hotel to what I thought would be the pavement and a town.

You could have knocked me down with another feather when I walked out onto a seafront promenade. I had no idea I was on the coast! Not only that it was the exact same picture as I had on my vision board, even including the picket-type fence along the walkway down to the beach!!!!!

Oh, and another very quick story …. My energy guided me to put "I wrote a book" onto my board in the 12-to-18-month section. I can absolutely guarantee that writing a book had never been on my radar at all and I never really thought any more about it.

As part of my business process, I was running my Get Focused Fast 5-day Challenge and one of the ladies in the group offered anyone to write a Chapter for her book, as a collaborating author, she needed a couple more to be able to finish the book. I thought "why not" and submitted a Chapter for her.

It only got to be an Amazon number one, best seller, internationally – in USA, UK and Canada!!!!! That was a bit of a celebratory Christmas lunch I can tell you, because it achieved number one on the 19th December!

Hopefully now you can see why I am so excited about Energy Vision Boards. The thing is these events keep continuing. Every time I have created a new one something magical has occurred in one form or another. I love holding the Energy Vision Board workshops because there is a mixture of joy and confusion as to what the final board means. Allowing my energy to be in flow has guided me on what to place on my boards and as I said earlier, I create them every 6 months as I and my energy evolve and grow.

If you would like to know more about Energy Vision Boards, please have a look at my website
www.stephaniethompsoncoaching.com

Getting back to Walt Disney's "If you can dream it, you can do it". Let me ask you –

o What is it that you really want to achieve?

o Does it encompass and guide everything you do?

o Is it your guiding light for all your decisions?

o Does it help you prioritise your day?

If the answer is "no" then possibly your vision is not compelling enough! "Hhhhmmmmm Stephanie", I hear you say, "what do you mean by compelling? It's something I want so that's it isn't it?"

Well no. Not really. Just wanting it is not enough. It needs to be all encompassing.

Let me share two extremes with you that will hopefully explain .....

Many years ago, when I was married, I found out my second husband was having an affair and it had been going on for some time. The two of us had gone on holiday to have some quality time together to try and sort things out. During this holiday I read a self-help book, Unlimited Power by Tony Robbins, which asked you to do various exercises. So, this particular day, whilst laying on the sunbed on the beach, I followed the instructions and it went a little like this ...

Think of a situation now make it bigger, brighter, noisier, louder, more colourful – look around you and see what is going on. Does that make you feel better?

I can assure you, imagining them cuddling, whilst doing this exercise was not good for my constitution in any way shape or form. If anything, it made me more furious! The power of the mind, you see?

Fortunately, I persevered with reading the book and moved onto the next exercise. Which said - think of a situation now make is smaller, duller, quieter, squeakier, black and white, in the distance – look around you and see what is going on. Does that make you feel any better?

Oh yes, it made me feel far, far better, especially as, metaphorically, I walked away and happened to step on the miniature squeak that I saw in my mind's eye!!!
In actual fact this particular exercise saved my marriage for a further eight years, but I digress, yet again. I said I might, didn't I?

Another example - during my many adventures through life I went to an Imax Theatre at one point. I don't know if that was just the name, or if it is a recognised name for a particular cinema. However. The screen was absolutely massive and you also sat very very close to the screen too. It filled your whole vision. It almost felt like you were sitting on the head of the person in front of you, quite a strange sensation. Then, when the film started, I have never experienced anything like it before! Because the screen was so big and the picture so colourful and the sound so loud, I actually felt like I was in the helicopter swooping over the tops of all the trees, weaving in and around the mountain sides! It was a phenomenal experience.

My point for sharing these two examples is to explain what I mean by compelling. Is your vision compelling enough? Does your 'big why' play like a movie in your head? Is it loud? Bright? Colourful? Does it fill your whole vision? Do you actually feel like you are in the picture yourself? Can you see it, hear it, feel it, taste it, smell it, touch it? Is it so all-encompassing, that you forget it is not real in that moment?

Here is a random example from my experiences. I did a guided meditation and at one point I was walking through New York, dressed in a tartan skirt and black patent pumps, I was walking to work, I could hear the cars driving past, taxis hooting and I could hear my shoes tapping on the pavement. I could feel the blow of wind as I walked over a subway grate. I could even smell candyfloss in the air as I walked towards the bakery to fetch my breakfast. I still remember that vision to this day and I can recall it instantly, it has never faded. It was so vivid! So real!

This is what I mean by compelling! Engaging every single one of your senses in to your vision!

Recall what I said earlier - the brain does not know the difference between imagination and reality - when we did the beach exercise? Well, this is why. Being able to live in your vision, your brain will believe it and start recognising things to show and prove you are achieving it. Then the more you recognise synchronicities, the more you will notice things supporting your vision.

Having your vision so compelling and all-encompassing will also influence the decisions you make, even simple ones like "shall I work on my social media content? Or shall I binge watch TV?" If your vision is deep-seated, within your psyche, it will help you stay focused and on track.

Another way of making your vision really compelling is to talk about it with as many people as possible. Share it far and wide, with friends and family. Enjoy having it as part of the conversation when you see them. Be excited to hear them ask "What is happening with you now?" "What are you doing with your business?" "What have you got coming up?" These are all questions they will ask and it will keep your big why at the forefront of your mind. Plus, you won't want to turn around and say "oh, no, I've decided not to do that anymore!" it will keep you focused and motivated. You will want to share how much progress you have made, what you have been up to, what is planned and what opportunities have come your way.

I've shared with you about old traditional vision boards and energy vision boards. Whether you decided to try an energy vision board is your choice. But I do recommend, now you have a deeper understanding of why your vision should be so compelling, that you have some form of meaningful, visual, representation. One that will keep you focused and give you the courage to take the necessary steps to achieve your dreams

So, let's assume you have created a vision board. Now what?

Well … I am quite curious about Feng Shui. I even chose the colour of my front door through Feng Shui, when I renovated my house! Anyway, before I digress any further, I did a bit of research and found out about Feng Shui Energy numbers and success corners. There is a calculation I found, to identify your Energy number, otherwise known as your Kua number, and subsequently your success corner. Now I don't want to contravene any copyrights at this point, so I will suggest you have a look on Thespruce.com, by Anji Cho, to do your calculation and then there is a link to take you through to determine your success corner direction too. I am sure there are many other sites that can assist identifying your Kua number too, this happens to be the one I used.
https://www.thespruce.com/what-is-a-feng-shui-kua-number-1275185

Once you have identified your Energy number and the direction of your success corner, you can go on to add Chinese symbols to enhance it even more. I'll let you do your own research, because I am no expert in this field at all! However, I will share I now have money turtles and money plants, amongst other things, residing happily in my success corner.

The reason why I am sharing all this? Because once I had identified my own success corner and also moved my vision board into it, my business absolutely flew. It took off big time and I have not looked back! I have attracted Ideal Clients, my income has expanded, my self-belief and self-motivation has increased, soooo many opportunities come to me it is just wonderful.

Another thing I want to share about "Is your big why compelling enough?" – it is not enough just to have a vision!

Paul McKenna quotes in his book "Change your life in 7 days" … "The Universe puts one more step in between you thinking of what you want and actually getting it – the action step".

It does not matter how big your dream is, as long as you take aligned action it will happen.

How to take aligned action?

For me, on a daily basis, I use the Energy Alignment Method (EAM) I spoke about earlier to ensure I am fully in flow with the layers of my aura, my chakras, the laws of the universe. That my head, heart and hara are in positive alignment and I am sending out one congruent message. Once I am fully in flow then I FOCUS to plan it, create it, believe it, offer it and prof-it.

How? I hear you ask.

Look at your 'big why' and decide when you want it fulfilled. For example, 5 years. Split your vision into smaller steps to be achieved during years 1, 2, 3, 4 and 5 to fulfil your vision. Now you have a 5-year plan.

Examples of steps, goals, targets you want to achieve include:
  o Number of clients
  o Amount clients pay
  o Type of clients you are attracting
  o Amount of turnover
  o Number of programmes offered
  o If you have a Virtual Assistant (VA)
  o Number of people in your business support team.

There are all sorts of goals you may want to focus on for different aspects of, or different stages of, your business.

The best bit of advice I can share at this point is - keep it simple. Yes, "what gets measured gets done!". However, if you make it too complex, especially when first starting up, you may spend more time measuring than actually making progress.

To continue with the 5-year plan - look at the first year and split that smaller goal across 12 months of actions. One action per month as a rough guide. Now you know what to achieve in each month of the year, to realise that first yearly goal.

If you wish you can even split the months into steps to take each week, even down to each day.

Remember, the time closest to you will have far more detail than 5 years hence. However, you can see the beginning of how you are going to realise your "big why".

Then, as time marches on, actions are taken and you achieve the first week, first month, first year, you repeat this exercise for year 2, then year 3. Before you know it, you will be approaching year 5 and your "big why" will be a reality. Which is the most fantastic feeling in the world.

My final piece of advice is, make sure you celebrate every step of the way. It is very, very, easy indeed to stay fully focused on the goal and forget just how far you have come. So, as you are making your weekly, monthly, quarterly plan make sure you plan in some celebrations too. I suggest the celebrations are linked to particular milestones, but not necessarily. Whatever you decide please do acknowledge what you have achieved. It will deepen your motivation to keep going and to achieve your compelling vision.

This reminds me of when I worked in the corporate world. There was a ladder of success I could get promoted through. My husband, at that time, set me incentives to achieve those rungs on the corporate ladder. It started with a weekend away at a nice hotel in the UK for the first rung.

The next incentive was to have an overnight stay at the Ritz in London. If we had gone the night before, Robbie Williams would have been there. We had a lovely meal and drank an expensive bottle of wine. We also drove down, because my husband wanted to step out of his car and hand the keys over for the car to be parked, so the visit enabled him to realise one of his dreams too. On the Sunday morning of our stay, we sat eating breakfast and my husband leant across to say the breakfast was very nice but he enjoyed my Sunday morning breakfasts more! Bless him.

The next rung on the ladder was to eat a Waldorf salad at the Waldorf Astoria in New York. I asked if we could defer the visit by a couple of months so that we could combine it with New Year celebrations too. We did eat the Waldorf Salad, which was lovely but what I remember most was the chicken soup pie. I make a turkey soup at Christmas, with the leftover turkey, that my daughters adore. It is very thick and creamy with lots of turkey and veg. Well, it was almost like the Waldorf had taken my turkey soup and put a pastry crust on the top. It was absolutely divine. And yes, we did see the New York New Year Celebrations Ball drop, in Times Square, too.

The final incentive was an overnight stay at Raffles in Singapore. We even had our own valet for the stay. Sooooo decadent. And yes, we drank a

Singapore Sling and were able to throw peanut shells on the floor. It is the only place you can throw litter in Singapore without getting fined!

By celebrating each promotion, I gained some amazing memories and I was able to see just how far I had come, before looking ahead to the next milestone. So, make sure you celebrate each and every success as you go through.

Oh and here is one final quick tip. Aim to complete three actions each day, to move your business forwards. Plan the night before what you want to achieve the next day and write each task on a post-it note. I love post-it notes!!! At the end of the day, you can tick them off, but don't throw the post-its away, keep them to one side. Complete those three tasks every day, watch those post-it notes mount up and get those addictive dopamine hits. Being addicted to the dopamine hits, by progressing your business, is a motivator in itself. At the end of the week, you will have 15 post-its in your pile. That's 15 steps you have progressed your business, so celebrate and enjoy the dopamine rush. Obviously, I am not suggesting a night away each weekend, although if you do then enjoy every moment. Your weekly celebration might come in the form of a dance around the kitchen table, or a curry on Friday night, or a drink in the pub. Whatever it is, make sure you acknowledge your achievements and successes of the week.

Keep those 15 post-it notes and repeat the planning for the following week, each day. And the following week and the one after that. THEN get the 4 weeks of post-its together. You will have 60 post-its!!!!!!. That means you will have moved your business forwards by 60 steps in that 4-week period. WOW that will be a massive dopamine rush!!!! What do you think to that?

As we draw to the end of stage one, hopefully, you have gained some insight as to:
- o Why it is essential to have a compelling vision that you can play like a movie in your head.
- o Where to place your vision board to enhance your success.
- o Why it is good to have a plan and measure achievements.
- o Why it is so good to celebrate each step of the journey.

I would love to hear about your success, so please do drop me a note to stephanie@stephaniethompsoncoaching.com

Also, if you have any questions, please send them to the same email address above.

When you are courageous, it inspires others to be brave.

Be that inspiration. Be fearless and take that step.

Chapter 3 –

Who do you want to work with?

"Like attracts like".

Look at your own group of friends and there are, more than likely, some similarities between you and them. Not everything, but enough to have built rapport from day one.

It is the same with clients. You will attract clients who resonate with you and your story.

Often you will hear the term Ideal Client Avatar or ICA, maybe you've heard "Soul Mate Client". When it comes right down to it, whatever term you use - they are the people you want to work with. There may be a number of different reasons for wanting to work with them too.

Maybe you suffered a physical, mental or emotional trauma, have survived and you don't want others to go through what you went through.

Maybe you are passionate about your hobby and you have a wealth of knowledge and experience that you want to share.

Whatever your reason for becoming a coach you want potential clients to resonate with you and you with them.

Two questions I am asked a lot:
- o "Who is my Ideal Client?"
- o "I've done the Ideal Client work, but now what do I do with it?"

Well let's start with "who is my Ideal Client". In short, YOU are your Ideal Client, at a point previously in your life. It could be when you went through a divorce, had children, changed from a corporate role to a self-employed role, experienced stress/anxiety/depression, experienced debt, experienced trauma/PTSD/ bereavement, experienced weight gain/weight loss, suffered a severe illness, the list goes on and on.

The reason why YOU are your Ideal Client is because you got through that time in your life and you are out the other side. You found what worked for you and you do not want others to experience what you had to go through so you want to share and save them the years of trial and error you went through till you found something that worked.

Alternatively, your Ideal Client may have the same interest as you, such as yoga, fishing, pilates, snooker, healthy eating, car mechanics, knitting, running, painting, cycling, ceramics, baking, jewellery making, a particular sport, dressmaking, computer gaming, cooking, gardening, the gym and this list also goes on and on. These are the things that you absolutely love doing and want to share your passion with others who have the same interest or want to learn about your interest.

Whatever topic you wish to coach then it is right for you.

Coaching is about sharing your passion, your experience, your knowledge or a combination. For me, I am passionate about business, I have experienced working in a variety of different sized companies and I have travelled the world to be trained by some awesome gurus such as Tony Robbins. I have received a number of both practical and academic business qualifications too. Therefore, I bring all three areas to my coaching clients.

You can approach identifying your Ideal Client Avatar (ICA) from two different angles. There is no right or wrong way, it is whatever fits best for you.

Please remember that as you evolve and grow your business then your Ideal Client Avatar (ICA) may also evolve and grow. This exercise is to establish who you are working with **for now**. The other thing to remember is that it does not have to be your whole life experience you share when talking about your story. Only share what you are comfortable sharing. It could just be one part of your life, a particular experience, a season in your life, or even just one day.

As an aside, I can tell you my 35th birthday was a huge turning point for me, it helped me become the woman I am today and that was just one day! I was nearing 35, I had been divorced for 5 years, I was bringing up my two gorgeous daughters, I was holding down a full-time job, I was studying at night school and I was Chairman of the Parent Teachers Association. I was in the tailspin of juggling, making sure everyone was happy and everything was done to a high standard. I stood in my kitchen that day, realised my 35th birthday was fast approaching and there was no-one to give me a birthday party! There was no-one to do something nice for me and make me feel special.

It was at that moment I realised I needed to make myself happy from the inside out. I realised it is not the 'things' in life that make us happy; it is how we feel on the inside. It was on that day I took the decision that changed the rest of my life. I was going to be happy and if I was unhappy about anything then I would change it.

Yes, I could have dived into a maelstrom of emotions feeling sorry for myself, blaming others, being angry with the world but I chose … I chose a vibrant life. One that has given me so many opportunities ….. like walking on hot coals. In fact, I liked doing that so much I done it twice more! …….. Breaking a plank with my bare hands. …..Climbing and jumping off the top of a 50m pole. Walking on glass and also breaking an arrow with my throat. I chose to improve my education mid-life focusing on business qualifications and now, have more letters after my name than in my name! I chose to take up an opportunity that randomly presented itself to me and within eight weeks I became a contributing author of a number-one international best-seller. None of these would have been realised had I not made the decision, on that fateful day, to make myself happy on the inside first.

Anyway, I digress, let me get back to 'who is your Ideal Client'.

Here is an exercise for you to determine who is your Ideal Client. Remember the more you put in the more you will get out.

I use this Ideal Client methodology all the time. I regularly end up with two flip-chart sheets FULL of answers when I do this exercise. Usually every six months, just so I am on track. I then put the results up on my kitchen wall, where I work every day, and I refer to it constantly when creating my social media posts. I use the information so I can tap into my Ideal Client's psyche. I can understand their pain, their quandary, their dreams so that, through my social media posts, I am always talking directly to them.

Another piece of advice, before we start the exercise - the more niche you go, the more clients you will attract. Being too broad means potential clients do not fully understand what you are offering. By niching it means you can get really focused and serve those clients well.

I will give examples to the questions, so you can see how I answer the questions from a coaching point of view. The questions can be applied to sharing your passion too. Let's get started ...

There are the standard questions like age, gender, marital status, if they have children, where they live, any pets, extended family, so let's skips the standard stuff which you can answer anytime and move onto the deeper questions.

1) Give 5 results that your client most desires.
My Ideal Client desires:
- o Clear, step-by-step guides on how to set up their business so it is as automated as possible and they have more freedom.
- o Simple successful strategies to attract paying clients to their business.
- o How-to videos to take away the tech headaches and they can get to it straight away.
- o Regular contact with me, to ask any questions.
- o Workbooks with clear explanation.
- o Access to materials 24/7, so they can work whenever they have time available.
- o A motivating, inspirational and supportive community, who understands what they are going through and can share their experiences.

2) Give 3 fears that stops your client in their tracks.
My Ideal Client is fearful of:
- o Being found wanting, of not being good enough.
- o Being visible and of others judging them.
- o Being found out as an imposter, who does not have the authority to share their teachings.

I know when I first started out as a coach, I certainly experienced all of these things. It is a natural cycle as we build our confidence and expertise. I am sure you have heard of the saying "feel the fear and do it anyway? I shared earlier how I have walked on hot-coals three times, broke a plank with my bare hand, climbed and jumped off the top of a 50meter pole. Walking on glass and broke an arrow with my throat. Having achieved all of these I have certainly felt the fear! However, now I have the attitude "well it's not putting anyone's life at risk, so let's try it". Believe me as I write ... as you overcome the fear you start to make progress.

Life is so much better one step past fear.

3) Give 3 challenges your client's face and what are the common symptoms they experience?

My Ideal Client challenges are:
o Sharing their story because it is too emotional for them.
o Overwhelm at sharing publicly what they have experienced.
o Being anxious about how family members will react.
o Procrastination and perfectionism which results in making no progress on their business at all.

To digress for a moment, I'll share my procrastination shame with you. I was a secretary back in the day and the Managing Director wanted a particular piece of paper, which they couldn't find. I confessed it was probably in the pile of filing on my desk. Quite a large pile, unfortunately. To my utter shame the next thing I know, the Managing Director was doing my filing and eventually found the piece of paper they were looking for. After that embarrassing incident, I always made sure I did not procrastinate on the filing, because I did not want to feel so mortified again! I was shamed out of a bad habit.

4) Give 3 mistakes your client is making

My Ideal Client makes the mistake of:
o Staying invisible, staying small.
o Letting their inner critic talk them out of taking action before they have even taken the first steps.
o Making decisions on behalf of their clients, which is a total dis-service.

We all make mistakes, nobody is perfect. In fact, I have a story about that too. Perfection is the lowest standard you can achieve! Why? Because no matter how perfect you make it, another person will want it in a different colour, or in a different format. They'll suddenly request that you add in something (that you hadn't even thought of!). Striving for perfection? You will never achieve it. Plus, it is also a form of procrastination and let me ask you this …… Which do you choose - procrastination or progression?

5) Give 3 things your client thinks they are doing right, but it's actually stopping them achieve their dreams.

My Ideal Client is:
o Making sure everything is perfect so others cannot criticise.

- Making sure they have their whole course ready to go, before venturing into sales

It can take hours and hours to create a course. What if nobody buys it? You have spent all those hours creating for no reward. It is far better to have a thorough outline of what the course is about and what it will achieve so you can talk about it. Then, once it is sold, you can actually create it.

- Looking at what everyone else is doing, under the guise of research and then suffering comparisonitis.

Comparisonitis? You know ... that paralysing situation where you have compared yourself to everyone else, then decided you have no idea what you are talking about. As a result, you come to the conclusion no-one will want to know what you have got to say. The final nail in the coffin is thinking no one will buy. I can assure you, right now, people DO want what you have to offer. It is all down to FOCUS - plan it, create it, believe it, offer it, prof-it.

I have just gone through 5 different questions that you can use to identify your Ideal Client Avatar. You will also find nuggets in answering these questions too.

6) What does your Ideal Client want?

My Ideal Clients want:
- To understand what to do, in what order.
- To understand how the process fits together.
- To sleep, whilst their business is earning money.
- To share their knowledge and expertise to help others grow and expand.
- To have a life full of freedom.
- To work their own hours.
- To support themselves financially, which ultimately brings them feelings of security.
- To have the freedom to work when and where they want.
- To feel wanted and listened to.
- To feel they are helping others.

Try to really identify what your Ideal Client wants and, if you can, also answer "why". Asking why helps you to delve deeper into your Ideal Client Avatar psyche too. Flip back to that last question and now you have those answers, ask why to drill down further.

6.a. What does your Ideal Client want?

My Ideal Clients want:

- o To understand what to do, in what order.
   Why? Because they are totally overwhelmed on how it all works.
- o To understand how the process fits together.
   Why? Because it just seems too complicated to get their head round.
- o To sleep, whilst their business is earning money.
   Why? Because life does not have to be hard work.
- o To share their knowledge and expertise to help others grow and expand.
   Why? So others do not go through what they went through.
- o To have a life full of freedom.
   Why? Because they have had enough of stress after being stuck in the hamster wheel of corporate work for so long.
- o To work their own hours.
   Why? Because they have had enough of the alarm clock ruling their life.
- o To support themselves financially, which ultimately brings them feelings of security.
   Why? Because they want to supplement their pension for the finer things in life, such as a trip to London and tea at the Ritz.
- o To have the freedom to work when and where they want.
   Why? So they can travel around the world and visit some awesome places
- o To feel wanted and listened to.
   Why? Because having been stuck in a corporate life they have forgotten who they are.

- o To feel they are helping others.
   Why? Because they want to be of service to others and feel worthy.

7) What is keeping your Ideal Client awake at night?

My Ideal Client does not know how to:

- o Plan her brand.
- o Create a logo.
- o Structure her business.
- o Attract her Ideal Client.
- o Create workbooks and visuals.
- o Capture email addresses.
- o Design and create a lead magnet.
- o Design and deliver a 3, 4 or 5-day low-cost valuable offer.

31

- o Design and deliver a signature programme.
- o Receive money.
- o Find her tribe.
- o Create raving fans.
- o Decide on a social media strategy.
- o Decide on a marketing strategy.
- o Manage business accounts.

There is nothing worse than lying awake at night mulling things over in your head! It causes stress and anxiety, which results in poor health. This is when having a mindset tool to use comes in handy. For me I use the Energy Alignment Method to clear resistances and bring in clear, calming thoughts, so I can move forward.

8) What does your Ideal Client suffer from?
My Ideal Client suffers from:
- o Overwhelm.
- o Fear of being judged.
- o Fear of being visible in the public eye.
- o Fear of being told they are not good enough.
- o Imposter syndrome.
- o Lack of confidence.
- o Lack of know-how.
- o Lack of clarity.
- o Lack of focus.
- o Lack of time.

It may be a combination of some or all of the above. When you go down the "fear of …" or "lack of …" route, the list can be endless! Again, I can use the Energy Alignment Method to release resistant energy and allow in confidence, clarity, focus and know-how.

9) What is at stage for your Ideal Client?
My Ideal Client is:
- o Frustrated they do not have enough time to get their coaching business established and money coming in before redundancy or retirement hits.
- o Anxious their health is suffering with all the stress in the day job, but not sure what to do first to get started with their coaching business.
- o Allowing themselves a year to get their coaching business established; the deadline is fast approaching, with no real progress made.
- o Frustrated that family and friends consistently say "get a proper job".

Once 'what's at stake' is determined, the information is invaluable for the creation of social media marketing posts.

Also the answers are showing if nothing changes for your Ideal Client this is what they are facing. By sharing your understanding, through your social media posts, they will know you "get" them, understand them and they begin to listen more. It is all part of building that magical rapport … connection with potential clients.

10) What's stopping your Ideal Client fix the problem themselves?
My Ideal Client:
- o Has a brain, is intelligent and knows how to make things happen, once they know where to start, but they don't really know what to do first. They have listened to all the gurus, made copious notes in an abundance of notebooks, they have papers all over the place with scribblings. But, at the end of the day, there is no real order, no clear plan to follow.
- o Feels overwhelmed by the choices and options available. They are looking for someone to join up all the dots.
- o Is bored and wants something to do to keep them occupied, but feels they are too old to do coaching and learn all the new technology etc.
- o Everything they need is within them now, they just do not realise it and so are regularly chasing shiny pennies. I'll reveal more about shiny pennies later in the book.

In our everyday lives there are some things we may not be able to do, for example mend a car, or fix a leaking pipe. In which case, we would call in an expert; a mechanic or a plumber. The same applies to coaching.

Your potential clients have a problem but they do not know how to fix it. As their potential coach the difficulty to overcome is they may not realise they have a problem OR that their problem can be fixed.

This is why it is so important to fully understand, in depth, who your Ideal Client is, what they think, feel, dream about. It all builds the picture to be able to talk with them and build that essential connection and relationship. It's the way to build rapport.

11) What will your Ideal Client's life look like, once they have worked with you?
My Ideal Client will:

- o Have a bespoke business structure in place, with as much of it automated as possible to allow them freedom
- o Have a clear pathway for client success
- o Have a clear pathway for business prosperity.

Through understanding what your Ideal Client wants, you can build your programmes to deliver their desired outcome. Being able to paint the picture, through your social media posts, of how their life will be in the future; it provides them with security that you understand what they are looking for and can help them.

12) Why should your Ideal Client buy from you?
This is the time to pick out key testimonials of what clients have said about working with you. For example;
- o "Working with Stephanie has been a game-changer. She is an expert in her field. She understands how to define your goals, take action and is supportive at the same time", shared by Tricia in New York, USA
- o "Steph taught me how to stay standing. She gave me the courage to change the things that needed to be changed and the serenity to let other things be. Everyone deserves a Steph in their lives", shared by Debra in Ohio, USA
- o "Stephanie's programme was just what I needed to get me started in getting my course out to the world. Laid out in concise simple steps, no fluff or beating about the bush, and Stephanie's warm delivery made each class easily digestible. I feel really confident now that I have a clear structure to get me working towards my business goals. Thank you, Stephanie, you are awesome!". Shared by Elaine in Italy. Unfrazzled and Unstuck.

Don't be ashamed of sharing what people have said about working with you. Yes, it may feel like you might be blowing your own trumpet but testimonials are confirmation that you can deliver results. It also supports your client's decision-making process – if someone has benefited from your guidance then they can benefit too.

Another set of questions to consider, when identifying with your Ideal Client, is to "walk in your client's shoes"

13) What do they think? Why do they think that?
- o My Ideal Clients thinks they can help people because they have a wealth of experience and knowledge to share.

14) How do they feel? Why do they feel that?
  o My Ideal Clients feel they are not good enough because they are floundering on where to start.

15) What are their fears and failures? Why are they afraid?
  o My Ideal Client fears failure because they do not have the confidence to become visible.

16) What are their hopes and dreams? Why are these hopes and dreams so important to them?
  o My Ideal Clients hopes and dreams of having a steady income so they can spend time with family doing the things they love.

17) Where are they right now? Why are they there?
  o My Ideal Client is stuck because they are overwhelmed by the amount of information and don't know who to listen to, or what to do first.

18) Where do they want to be? By when? Why do they want that?
  o My Ideal Clients wants to have a stress-free life, with boundaries between work and pleasure. They want to start right now and see progress in their business because they feel time is running out.

There is a lot of power in asking the question why. In fact, it is a recognised tool to use when understanding a problem.

It can be very frustrating when you are on the receiving end of "why" but it is an extremely powerful little word. Think about a small child, often they go through a phase of asking "why" and they just keep asking. Their parent starts off on solid ground but as the child digs deeper it really makes their parent stop and think.

If you want to get into the depths of your Ideal Client then keep asking the question "why". Oh and by the way, usually when you have asked "why" 5 times you are at the point of discovery, rarely do you need to ask more than 5 times.

And the final set of questions to answer are from your own perspective as their potential coach.

19) Why should they work with me?

- o Because I give personal attention to helping my clients create a simple business model, that is as automated as possible, so they can live their dream live.
- o I share my wealth of knowledge and experience willingly.
- o I am patient in answering questions and ensure my clients have full understanding of where they are going, why they are doing things and how to take the action to achieve them.
- o I take time to fully understand their dreams and aspirations, so I can support them fully.
- o I have very loyal clients who are willing to share their experience of working with me. (The testimonials you gather as you work with friends, family and clients are just that – a testimony to what you can achieve for them).

20) Why should they be interested in this programme?
- o Because I provide clear, step-by-step guides, with supporting how-to videos and templates etc to overcome their technophobia.
- o Because I am conscious of balancing work and life, my how-to videos are in short bite-sized chunks, so they can even progress their business during the lunch hour.
- o Because I provide a one-stop-shop with quick and easy access, so they can learn and implement at a time to suit them.

21) Why should they purchase now, what difference will it make? Or, if they don't start now then what will change?
- o If you always do, what you've always done. You'll always get what you've always got. It's time to cast your net elsewhere.

What I teach in my programmes is exactly what I did, or do, in my own business that resulted in my becoming an international coach, this is why I can say the methods I teach are tried, tested and get results.

I share step-by-step all the methods, systems and processes that worked for me. This means my clients do not have to experience shiny pennies syndrome. Clients can get a head start on where I began in my business. They do not have to experience all the false starts either, which saves tons of money believe me!

I took a moment once to work out how much I had invested in my journey to becoming a successful coach, when I got to £50,000, I stopped counting!

I also took the opportunity to reflect on all my learnings. It distils down into ten key things. Ten things that need to be in place for a successful coaching business and that is how I designed my coaching business. Start with the ten key steps, get really established and build further from there.

I mentioned shiny pennies and there is a story to tell. I think you'll like it; I know I did when I first heard it, shared by Keith Cunningham. See if this metaphor story resonates with you ....

You are standing at the back of the queue at the deli counter. When you get to the front of the queue there will be lots of choice - cheese, ham, pies, olives, bread, etc. You will have an abundance of things to choose from – once you get to the front of the queue.

You stand in line and you are slowly moving towards the front of the queue. But then something catches your eye. You see some lovely smoked salmon (otherwise known as a shiny penny) in one of the fridges. So, you decide to go and have a look. Hmmmm it is not quite what you are looking for. Never mind and you go back to the deli counter. The only thing is that you have to go to the back of the queue. You cannot jump into the queue where you were before, you have to start all over again.

Again, you stand in line, slowly moving forwards to what you really want. But something catches your eye again. This time you can see a beautiful chocolate and cream gateau in a different fridge (another shiny penny). You go to have a look. Hmmmm it is still not quite what you are looking for. Not to worry, you can go back to the deli counter, you have only been gone a couple of minutes. The queue has grown and you have to start all over again, you cannot jump in where you left.

Now look at your business. Look at what you have been doing over the past year. How many times have you gone chasing shiny pennies, different promises by other coaches? And then when you have tried to come back to where you were, you find you have to start all over again, because you have lost momentum with your community, your clients, your message, possibly even no longer resonate with what you were building and have to go right back to the beginning again.

You have to pick up all the threads again. You need to try and remember why you did that post. Have to remember how to do the website pages, the landing pages, check the links are all working. The list goes on. All because you went chasing after shiny pennies.

Don't worry, I was just as guilty when I started out with my coaching! It took me a while to realise that I should choose one or two gurus and follow them. Choose ones that resonate with me, that I feel comfortable with, that I trust and believe in and who I believe will get me the results I desire.

The other vital, essential, mandatory, missing ingredient? The commitment to take action and implement what is being taught.

"Have a dream, have a plan and take aligned action to put the plan into play".

I know it is very easy to say, and a whole other ball game to make it happen, but now you are aware of the shiny pennies syndrome hopefully you will take a long hard look, choose one or two guru's that really resonate and stick with them. Just know the magic comes when you do actually implement their teachings.

The second question I am regularly asked is …

"I've done the Ideal Client work but now what do I do with it?"

The answer is "start with the end in mind". Now you have completed the Ideal Client work you will be able to reflect, see where your client is currently, learn what it is your client is trying to achieve. The latter is otherwise known as the outcome.

Once you know the outcome, you can design your programme so that it, and your client's outcome are the same. Please note, at this point there is no need to actually create the material, but you do need to know the outline (what and how you are going to teach it) and the outcome.

Based on the outline of the content of your programme you can decide on the lead magnet to use, to attract clients into your course. It is essential the programme and the lead magnet are supportive of each other, otherwise if may affect sales.

My favourite story to explain this is … a solicitor decides that he is going to deliver a course on how to draw up your own Will, but he is pondering on what to use for a freebie. His wife comes back from yoga and after a bit of discussion she suggests a meditation – all her friends love a meditation.

Great, he has his freebie and he has his course. The unfortunate thing is the meditation is not connected to how to draw up a Will and therefore where he is hoping to make sales they do not happen.

My reason for sharing this story is to explain you need synergy between your freebie and your course. One needs to lead smoothly into the other, so the client sees the benefit of progressing their learning with you further. It is all about building that trust.

Your lead magnet may have two stages. For example, a valuable free download pdf document followed by an interactive low-cost (or free) valuable offer of a few days; often five days, but it can be three, it can be ten. The length of time is dependent on what you are trying to help your potential clients achieve in that period of time. One day may not be long enough; ten days may be too long; you know what you want to achieve for your clients and how you are going to deliver it to enable that transformation.

Do also consider how much time your Ideal Client has available. If they are busy mums, trying to build a side business then they possibly cannot spare an hour at 6.30 pm every evening for a week – it's usually bath and bed time for a start.

Offering a 3, 5 or even 10 day low cost (or free) valuable offer is your ideal opportunity to build that "know, like and trust" with your potential clients.

Remember,
if they know and like you, they will listen,
it is only once they trust you, will they buy.

Seeing you in bite-sized sessions, over a few days, potential clients get to know you and decide if they want to work with you. Being live by offering a free, or low-cost, valuable masterclass/challenge/mini-course is the quickest way to build rapport and trust.

Which, in turn, increases your chances of converting their interest into a sale.

Once you know your freebie, and if you are going to do a free, or low-cost, valuable offer then it is down to your marketing strategy. This is where all the hard work and depth of understanding you have gained, from your Ideal Client Avatar work, comes into its own.

Look back through your Ideal Client answers and hopefully you will start to see some common themes. For example, my Ideal Client:-
- o knows they can help people but are overwhelmed by the amount of information to choose from
- o does not know where to start setting up their coaching business
- o is lost in the humdrum of their day-to-day life
- o cannot find time to focus on what they want to achieve
- o wants to attract clients but doesn't know how
- o wants financial freedom
- o wants to walk towards their dreams following a clear pathway with all the templates and how-to videos to help them do it as easily and quickly as possible
- o wants to automate as much as possible so they have freedom to do the other important things in their lives such as travelling, spending time with family and friends.

When creating marketing posts, use the words from your Ideal Client work and take your client on a journey, starting with their pain point and showing them what life could really be like (the pleasure point) if they work with you. Please note the whole journey does not have to be shared in every post. It could be you split the story over a series of posts throughout a week or a month.

Every piece of information you have gleaned from the Ideal Client Avatar work will:-
- o help potential clients identify with you
- o help them realise you "get them", that you get what they are going through
- o help them realise you really know them. And you know what? You do. Because it was you! Remember I shared earlier ...

YOU are your own Ideal Client.

You can talk about the pain you have gone through, during your own journey, to get to this point, what life is like now and the joy of being in this new place in your life.

My final piece of advice is about the marketing of your freebie, low-cost offer, course/programme, in fact anything you offer ... ensure it takes your client on a journey, from their pain point to their happy point. Using your own journey to happiness helps them realise there is an answer to their current unhappiness/ problem.

Talking of passion - My father has been a commercial grower all his life; growing plants is his vocation. Every so often my parents would go to the "Growers Meeting", which was all the local growers from the surrounding counties. Whilst they were in this environment, with like-minded souls, they would share their challenges and experiences. My father achieved a very very high germination rate when he grew from seed. Others didn't. So, he shared what he did; he took them on his journey sharing the success points so they could learn more quickly to gain the results he achieved.

Exactly as I am sharing with you today – he took them on his journey to help them get to the end point quicker; to go further faster.
As we draw to the end of stage two, hopefully, you have gained some insight on various aspects, including:

- o Identifying your Ideal Client through answering a number of questions.
- o You see how the information gleaned can support whilst creating marketing posts.
- o You are aware of shiny pennies syndrome and will make your decisions accordingly.

I would love to hear about your success, so please do drop me a note to stephanie@stephaniethompsoncoaching.com

Also, if you have any questions, please send them to the same email address above.

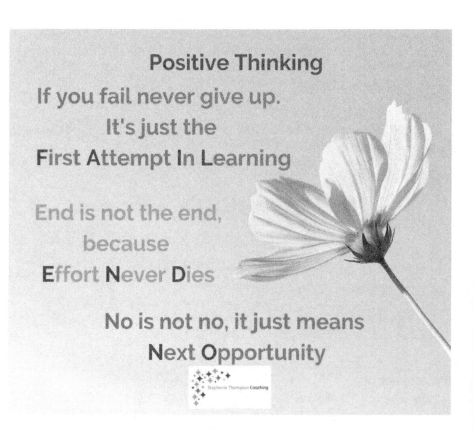

Positive Thinking
If you fail never give up.
It's just the
First Attempt In Learning

End is not the end,
because
Effort Never Dies

No is not no, it just means
Next Opportunity

Stephanie Thompson Coaching

42

Chapter 4 –

How do clients get to know you?

Well, to be obvious, your Ideal Client gets to know you through what you share of your journey; from your hell point to your heaven point.

I appreciate the words "Ideal Client Avatar" is very impersonal, so you may be having trouble identifying with your client. Might I suggest you give your Ideal Client a name; even add a picture from a magazine, so the words on the pages begin to have a personality? The picture is purely to act as a prompt for you. Don't worry no-one else is going to see the picture you use! As long as the image is meaningful to you and you feel connected to your client. I will confess, my own ideal client image is Fern Britton. She helps me no-end when I write to my ideal clients and she helps me stay focused.

Having identified your Ideal Client and answered the questions in the previous Chapter, you can now describe
- o what they are feeling right now
- o what is their hell

And by the same token, you can also describe
- o where they want to get to
- o how they want to feel when they get there - their heaven.

Keep these points firmly at the front of your mind when creating your marketing posts. Especially the heaven points, because they inspire your Ideal Client to realise what is achievable. The hell and heaven states are two vital pieces of information, as you share your stories, to build rapport with your potential clients.

To avoid stress and strain, to be authentic, vulnerable and transparent when sharing your stories – speak, or write, from the heart.

Share the emotions you experienced – the ups AND the downs. Help your Ideal Client really identify with you – because they are going through the exact same thing right now. Plus, by speaking authentically means your communications will be consistent and the rapport will build genuinely.

Just digressing slightly ... I remember when I worked in HR, I would go into meetings with lots of technical engineering jargon. It did not come easily to me, but it did to the rest of the attendees. In fact, it came that easily, they spoke in 3 letter acronyms!!! I remember going home to my husband after a particularly difficult day of technical meetings saying "They are talking another language! I have no clue what they are on about!".

My solution? To create my own dictionary in the back of my notebook of what the acronyms were and their meanings. It wasn't until about 6 months later I found there was a corporate dictionary, for just that purpose, so I gave a huge sigh of relief and was eventually able to hold my own in the conversations.

And then I changed roles. "No problem" I thought "the 3 letter acronyms will still be the same". Oh no!!! In some instances, yes, but sometimes the same 3 letters meant something totally different!

After 17 years, as I was leaving the company, they were starting to use FOUR letter acronyms! Heavens knows what headaches those combinations would cause!

Anyway, there is a message I am sharing in this story. Make sure you don't use too much, and I say this in inverted commas, "technical jargon" in your messages. For example, you may talk about "divine feminine". However, if you are introducing clients to the "divine feminine", they may not yet realise the "divine feminine" work is what they need. So, to capture their attention, you might use alternative words such as nurture, intuition, empathy (or what is relevant to your message) and then, in your programme, you can introduce them to the terminology "divine feminine" as they learn more.

And this is why I say it is really important to first know who your Ideal Client is. Because you tailor your message to their current "hell" state and your programme takes them on the journey to where they want to be and how they want to feel; the "heaven" state. If your Ideal Client is someone already "in the know" then using "technical jargon" is not a problem.

At the end of the day, it is all about being consistent, sustainable and authentic with your message, in relation to where your client is currently.

Back to the topic in hand - Did you know there are some magical words you can use in your messaging? Would you like to know what they are?

"...so that..."

Yes, that's it! "...so that..."

Allow me to explain ...

Reflecting on your Ideal Client work in the earlier Chapter ... what is the emotion your client is wanting to achieve? If everything was right in their world, what would the future look like? More freedom? More time? More money? Do they want support in understanding what they are going through? Do they want to gain knowledge? Do they want to feel stronger? Empowered? Confident?

And this is where the magical words "...so that/so they can..." comes in when formulating your message.

I help [*insert client*]
to [*insert the outcome*]
so that they can [*insert achieve your desire*].

Let me apply the formula and show you how it works with my own message, in a very simple format.

I help "life coaches"
to "reclaim time in their day and get focused fast"
so that they can "attract paying clients".

Ultimately my Ideal Client wants to have the time to concentrate on creating her business and attract paying clients to her programmes. Do you see how the formula works?

If you have a look on my website www.StephanieThompsonCoaching.com you will see how this formula crops up time and time again in one format or another.

Focus on the outcome of working with you, rather than the mechanics of what you will do during the programme.

Let me share the formula, with the magic words, again ....

I help [*insert client*]
to [*insert the outcome*]
so that they can [*insert achieve your desire*].

If you do not feel you have enough information in the Ideal Client Avatar work from a previous Chapter, then maybe you could do some journaling against these next few questions, to expand further ...

- o Who does my Ideal Client want to be?
- o What do they truly desire?
- o Why is that important to them?
- o What do they want to do?
- o If they got this, what would be different about their life?
- o What do they want to have?
- o What solutions are they looking for so badly that they are willing to pay?
- o What do they truly want to feel?
- o What do they want to stop feeling?
- o Why does your Ideal Client want what you are offering?
- o What's in it for them?

To get back on track, the original question was "how do clients get to know you"? It is achieved by sharing your story, by becoming an actual person in their eyes, by allowing them to get to "know, like and trust" you; through being transparent, being human and by being vulnerable. In other words, by being YOU.

Remember, not everything is perfect (despite what it might say on the social media platforms). Everyone tries different approaches, until they find a message that works for them which resonates with their Ideal Client.

In fact, that reminds me of when I first met my second husband. It was not a conscious decision but somehow over the first month of us living together, I never cooked the same meal twice! This particular day, and I have no idea why because I don't even like peppers, I decided to cook "stuffed peppers". Well out of the 30 odd meals that I had cooked over the month, this one was a bit of a disaster. It was bland and tasteless to say the least. I am a really good cook normally but this particular dish alluded me.

What I'm trying to allude to is - nothing is ever perfect. Be honest with your clients. If it is the first time you are running a particular programme then tell them so. Offer the programme at a slightly reduced amount - as there may be some bugs in the smooth running of the system, or there might be something that takes longer (or shorter) than you had planned. If you tell them up front, if you are open and honest, there will be more support and collaborative feedback.

And if something doesn't work? C'est la vie! Laugh about it. Learn from it. And uplevel.

There are some things to do BEFORE you begin to write your story and that is having a positive mindset and to be 'in flow'.

By having your energy aligned, and being in a high-vibration place, your message will flow smoothly, the right words will come and you will connect with your Ideal Client more easily.

Also, coming from a place of authenticity and serving (rather than a place of lack and needing), your message will resonate more, connection will be made and the "know, like and trust" journey can begin.

For me personally, to align my energy and get into flow, I use the Energy Alignment Method (EAM), originated by Yvette Taylor, where you use your whole body to sway in answer to what is going on in your energy. You sway forwards for a positive response, because you are moving towards; and you sway backwards for a negative response, because you are moving away. This is how it works …

Firstly, make sure there is nothing in front, or behind you, that you could stumble over, if you experience an exaggerated sway. Ideally stand in a quiet environment, ideally facing an open window. This technique can be used sitting down, even laying down, but the sway is not as strong.

Close your eyes. Shake out your shoulders, arms, body and legs. Stand with your feet hip-width apart and relax everything down; nothing clenched or tight. Take some nice deep, slow breaths and relax everything down. Come out of your head, and breathe into your heart. When you feel totally relaxed, say "my name is (*state your name*)" and feel your body sway forwards, showing a yes.

Then you can check your "no" sway by asking "my name is (*state another name*)". Congratulations, you have now tapped into your energy.

On the assumption that your sway is true (forwards for yes and backwards for no) here is a very brief taster for you to experience this modality.

Ask out loud "Do I have any resistant energy in the layers of my aura?".

If you swayed backwards for "no" then no further work is needed.

If you swayed forward for "yes" then recite this statement out loud. "I am ready to release any and all resistant energy, from the layers of my aura, right now. I release it from my energy in all forms, on all levels, at all points in time". Repeat this full statement 3 times.

Take a big breath in and blow all the negative energy out through all the layers of your aura.

Now check-in by asking the original question "Do I have any resistant energy in the layers of my aura?".

Please bear in mind this is a very brief example of using EAM however, fingers crossed you should now sway backward for "no". If not and you would like assistance in clearing your energy, so you are in flow, information can be found on my website www.stephaniethompsoncoaching.com

To continue with the EAM technique, and assuming you have now cleared the negative energy, we want to fill the gap with positive energy, so it lifts your vibration.

At this point, when working with a client I would ask for their input regarding what positive statements they want to include. However, I am going to share a short positive-vibe example to assist.

Stand with your arms outstretched and up and you feet hip width apart. This is to create funnels top and bottom to captures all the positive energy coming in from the Universe and the earth. I will warn you, right now, your arms get really heavy as the positive energy comes flooding in. So, close your eyes and repeat this statement 3 times … "I am ready to allow joy and love to flow through me, to be fully aligned with my message and to be 100% in flow. I allow this into my energy, right now, in all forms, on all levels, at all points in time".

Take a big deep breath in and, as you slowly exhale, slowly lower your arms, bringing all that amazing positive energy down; down through your head, through your heart, into your hara where creation is manifested, feel that positive energy going down your legs, into the ground, totally grounding you and bring your hands onto your heart where you feel the joy and love you have just allowed in.

Take a moment to centre yourself, then open your eyes and we will finish the EAM technique with some self-care advice.

This was a very brief introduction to EAM however you may well have experienced a big shift in your energy. The result is you may feel quite tired for the rest of the day. Be kind to yourself. Drink lots of water. Try to avoid alcohol. And get an early night's sleep.

The next steps to clearing your energy to get fully in flow, I would lead you through clearing the layers of your aura, your chakras, the laws of the universe; check that your head, heart and hara are in positive alignment and you are sending out one congruent message. More information can be found on my website
www.stephaniethompsoncoaching.com

Back to the topic of the Chapter ... once your energy is positively aligned what do you write about? Well, you write about YOU. But which part I hear you ask ... whichever part of your story will resonate with your Ideal Client the most.

This sounds simple and straightforward, however deciding can be a cause of great procrastination, so let me share how I overcome this situation.

I use mind-maps.

I get a roll of brown paper, or old wallpaper. Lay it across my kitchen table. Grab some coloured pens and begin by writing my Ideal Client in the middle of the sheet. I draw spurs off and label them with the various emotions my Ideal Client is experiencing now in their "hell" state. The information you need is in your Ideal Client work from a previous Chapter.

I then complete the next layer of information by taking the first spur and writing down all the times I have experienced that emotion AND I also write down all the things I did to counteract it.

Me being me, who loves a post-it and coloured pens, I would use the coloured pens so I could differentiate what information belonged to which spur. Believe you me, because you are totally in flow and attuned to your Ideal Client, once you start there is no stopping you. You will fill the whole sheet!

Continue working like this until you have information for each of the original spurs you wrote on the sheet. This exercise now reveals when you have experienced the emotion and also how you overcame it. It becomes a massively valuable piece of paper because not only is this the source of stories to tell, but it is also the beginning of the programme you can deliver to help your client move from their "hell" to their "heaven".

In this example I used emotions, however you can do the same for thoughts and also beliefs.

Effectively, through your stories, your Ideal Client is identifying with the emotions they are currently experiencing and can see there is an answer to where they want to be. You are sharing different stories around their emotions, thoughts and beliefs that will begin to show that you really know what they are going through and therefore can help them overcome these difficulties they are experiencing.

You can draw a second mind-map, again with your Ideal Client in the middle with different spurs off with headings such as:

  o Support options - who is around them, where they could go for help.
  o Self-care - how they can make themselves feel better.
  o Activities – actions they can take to keep motivated and focused.

These two mind-maps now become a source of social media posts which are still relevant to your Ideal Client moving out of "hell" into their "heaven".

The ultimate aim is that your story, your messages, your interaction with your Ideal Client at any point throughout the "know, like and trust" journey is relevant to them. It means something to them. It helps them identify with you.

Remember,
if they know and like you, they will listen,
it is only once they trust you, will they buy.

By staying focused in your communications means your Ideal Client will identify with you. You are showing empathy for where they are and inspiration to where they could be. Remaining consistent and on topic with your message build confidence in your Ideal Client. You become their guiding light and show things can, and do, get better.

So, do make sure you paint a picture of what life is like on the other side, not just what they are experiencing now, because that end picture is what they are actually wanting to achieve and you are showing how you can help them get there.

In this day and age of modern technology, there are many ways of communicating with your Ideal Client, such as Instagram, Facebook, Twitter, LinkedIn, Pinterest to name but a few. I am sure there are many others too. The thing is you don't want to burn yourself out. Of course, you are enthusiastic and willing to put the hours in, I accept that. HOWEVER, you cannot be "all things to all men" as the saying goes. The best piece of advice I can give you at this point is the Four Ones …

One client
One message
One platform
One call-to-action.

One Client – when you niche down and speak to one specific person you will get far greater connection than trying to speak to everyone about everything. I totally accept, as coaches, we can help many people, however niching is important, especially if you are just starting out as you are establishing yourself as an expert in your field. Plus, it avoids confusion for your potential clients and for you too.

One Message – be very clear on what you offer. Yes, you can help them in multiple areas of their life, but niche down to one particular area so they can really identify with you. Become the expert in that field; become the go-to person.

One Platform – when first starting out, everything is new and there is a very steep learning curve. Trying to juggle several social media platforms and all their idiosyncrasies at the same time may just be the last straw. Take a long hard look at where your Ideal Client hangs out and stick with that one platform to share your message. Once you have got it fully established, and automated where possible, then you can add another platform. Get that platform established, then add another one. Build up to it. Going "big bang" on all the social media platforms at once, you are going to spread yourself so thinly your message may get lost. Remember, it's not just putting your posts out, you also need to build a relationship with these wonderful potential clients, by responding to their posts and engaging in conversation with them. A quick click to "like" is not enough. For a start it counts more if you click to "love" and that click does not actually build a relationship. Remember, you want to build the "know, like and trust". How will they get to know you if you just click "love"?

One Call-to-action – a confused client never buys. When you are communicating with your potential clients, and it is appropriate, then include a call-to-action, but only one. You may feel you are being very helpful by saying "message me, or put a comment below, or email me, or sign up here" however the buyer gets confused and so takes no action at all. My advice, after trial and error, have one clear call-to-action.

Let's reflect on the book so far and allow me to point out I am sharing lots of different tools and techniques to get your online coaching business started. I am not doing just that though, am I? I am also interspersing my message with snippets about myself, by sharing different stories from my life. I am helping you get to know me; I am trusting you are getting to "know and like" me because I am sharing knowledge on something that you want to achieve. Ultimately, I believe, little by little, your trust in me will grow. You will want to know more about me and how I can help you. I will become a person to you and people buy from people they know!

There is another way of building rapport with your potential Ideal Clients and that is by sharing your knowledge and experience totally free, via a lead magnet. For example, you can download the "10 Steps To Conquer The Overwhelm, Reclaim Time In Your Day And Get Focused Fast" guide from my website
www.stephaniethompsoncoaching.com.

More about lead magnets later in the book.

Let's change focus for a moment and look at you, rather than your Ideal Client.

Absolutely, categorically, you must believe in yourself!
o   Believe in what you are doing.
o   Believe in the outcomes you can achieve for your clients.
o   Believe in your ability to deliver.
o   Believe in your worth.
o   Believe in the value you bring to your clients.

The key to success is knowing why you are doing what you do and how good you are at doing it! If you don't then your negative inner critic could cripple you! Also, think of it this way, if you don't believe in yourself, then how can your clients believe in you?

Choose your stories and be comfortable with the detail you are sharing, so your message flows easily and your clients can identify with you.

Choose your stories where you are sharing your authority, which also enables your Ideal Client to have confidence in you (this is not necessarily qualifications and certificates).

I could be quite disparaging here, but I am not going to be, I am just going to share the facts ….

My full name is Stephanie Ann Thompson, which is quite a long name I think you will agree? I have more letters after my name than in my name! I have post graduate and Masters Degrees that contribute to this. So what? It means I can regurgitate a text book! It means I can study and retain information. It does NOT necessarily mean that I can actually do the work.

Let me share this bit with you. I hold national vocational qualifications at Levels 2, 3 and 4. I also hold an Assessors qualification AND an Internal Verifiers qualification. Now not a lot of people rate NVQs (often referred to detrimentally as Not Very Qualified). However, there is something very particular about National Vocational Qualifications. They are not just a qualification on what you know, but a qualification on what you can DO as well. To complete an NVQ you need to demonstrate doing the actual tasks, as well as sharing your theoretical knowledge.

Let me share this further bit of information with you. Here are some testimonials of what people have said about working with me …..

"Hi Steph, I've just started going through your Masterclass and I can't tell you how helpful the knowledge you're sharing is to me. I'm about to set up my business and this information is exactly what I need. I'm so glad I signed-up to your membership!" This was from Jackie Lawrence of p-factorcoaching.com

Another?

"I have been working with Stephanie on her programmes over the last few months. I cannot praise her enough. Her knowledge and enthusiasm is infectious. I have always felt confident in my business experience but the coaching Stephanie shares is brilliant. She has made me up my game, I can now see a work life balance that I never had before. I will make sure I take part in all Stephanie's courses as I learn and grow so much. Make sure you follow this talented lady as she soars higher and higher". This was from Pearl Cox of Pearls of Wisdom.
https://t4s.site/pow-pearls-of-wisdom-ltd/home/

Now let me ask you this … As a potential client, which coach would you be most likely to work with? The one with all the qualifications, or the one that gets results? For me personally, it would be the one that gets results, because ultimately, as a client, this is what I am looking for – the results.

When sharing your stories be transparent, human and vulnerable. As I said earlier, not everything is perfect and sharing that vulnerability shows you are a human being. Someone your potential clients can identify with, because at the end of the day no one is perfect. We are all human beings.

So let me re-iterate what I said earlier … Choose your own stories where you are sharing your experience (good and bad) and what worked best for you. This establishes you as an authority who knows what they are talking about – because they have experienced it. This also enables your client to have confidence in you. I have mentioned in a previous Chapter this does not necessarily mean qualifications and certificates.

The other thing I said earlier was … choose your story and be comfortable with the detail you are sharing, so your message flows easily and your client can identify with you.

One of those negative inner voices you will probably have to fight is "why would anyone be interested in my story?", "what will those involved in my story have to say?", "what will people think of me?". These are all to do with the fear of visibility and you can certainly work on that, using the Energy Alignment technique I shared with you earlier. You can book a session with my, via my website www.stephaniethompsoncoaching.com if you are stuck with negative inner voices. I am delighted to say that since doing the work on myself, using this method, my inner critic is totally silent and it is bliss because boy was it noisy earlier in my life!!!!!

When sharing your stories, it does NOT have to be your whole life story, it could be a particular event, a day, a year, a relationship. You do not have to "air all your laundry in public" either! Choose the bits that are relevant to where your client is now (their "hell") and where they want to be (their "heaven") with a bit of what happened in between too. Share your own journey from your hell to your heaven, the ups and the downs and how you feel now the transformation has been achieved.

If you find that your story is going on for pages and pages (remember the attention span now-a-days is about 8 seconds before people scroll on) then use "cliff hanger" endings. What do I mean by that? Here is an example –

You are watching a box set on Netflix. You come to the end of the first episode and it leaves you hanging. You are left sitting on the edge of your seat. You look at the clock and decide you will just watch the start of the next episode to see what happens otherwise you won't sleep. And what happens? Before you know it, it's 2 o'clock in the morning, you've got work in the morning and you have to force yourself to go to bed! And then?!!!! You do it all over again the next night!

...... because they finish their episodes on a cliff-hanger!

You can do the same with your stories. Even ask the reader to leave an emoji in the comments if they want you to tag them into the next exciting instalment.

The more engaged you can become with your Ideal Client, and the more your client becomes engaged with you, the more the "know, like and trust" relationship will grow and you will bond. Then, before you know it, they will be buying your programmes.

I spent many years in the corporate engineering world, and my written word became conditions to that corporate way of communicating. Facts and figures. Black and white. Report writing etc. My written word was very official, directive, matter of fact! However, when you are building a relationship with your client this method of writing does not induce emotion and connection. So, my tip to you is, when you are creating your posts and copy, write as if you are talking to them, over a coffee or herbal tea, sat in your lounge. Remember I said in an earlier Chapter to choose a picture to represent your clients (mine was Fern Britton)? Well this is why. Write your posts as if you were chatting with them rather some unknown person out in the ether.

As I sit here writing, I can hear you say "yes Stephanie, but when I am sat in-front of the computer and I start typing I seem to go into this impersonal fog"! In answer I would suggest you look for an app you can use, where you sit, talk and the app writes what you say. You can even go into google docs and switch on the microphone so it types as you speak.

The joy of such technology, means you can grab a coffee (or tea) take your laptop or phone and sit down and chat away to a friend (in person or even metaphorically) and the laptop will write it all down. No need to worry about your brain overtaking and going into "official speak". And just think, you have actually had some time to sit in a nice place and enjoy your surroundings too. Win win all round.

Yes, I admit, you do then have to edit, but you would do that anyway regardless of how you got your story on paper. Also, if you want to write a book and have difficulties writing you could speak into one of these apps and then ask someone else to edit for you. Job done!

The posts you share should really answer one, or all, of 3 questions:
o   Why me?
o   Why this?
o   Why now?

Why me? – this is where you are sharing about you, who you are, what you have been through, how you have come out the other side. Why you are an expert in your field.

Why this? – this is where you are sharing about what worked for you, how it made such a difference to your life, where you are now, how far you have come, what life is like now you have come out the other side.

Why now? – this is where you share what happens if they don't take action now. That nothing will change and everything will be the same in one, three, five years' time. Suggest they do not want to look back in a years' time and wish they had started today. This information is in the Ideal Client Avatar work you did earlier in the book.

Here's a quick example ...

"Why me" section - I was always chasing after shiny pennies. I wanted to be a coach, I had the skills, I could achieve the transformations for my friends and clients but I just could not get my business up and running to attract paying clients. I was working with friends and family and occasionally friends of friends for a small donation of funds, but there was no real structure to my business, no systems in place, no plan!

"Why this" section – And then it all changed. I finally stopped chasing the shiny pennies and stuck with one coach. I listened to what she said and I implemented everything she taught me. I followed her step-by-step plans. I finally knew what I was doing and why I was doing it. It made a massive difference.

"Why now" section – I am now a number one, international, best-selling, contributing author, I have appeared on BBC television and BBC Radio, I am an international radio presenter, I have clients all over the world from New Zealand and Australia, across Europe, the UK and coast to coast in the USA. All this because I stuck with one coach and IMPLEMENTED what she taught. I teach my clients the exact same steps that I took, and still take, in my business to get where I am today, I share workbooks, templates, how-to videos, worksheets, how to automate as much of the business as possible and advise many many places to promote your programmes once you are ready to launch. If you would like to know more about working with me please email stephanie@stephaniethompsoncoaching.com

Anyway, let's move on to where and how you can show up to allow potential clients to get to know you.

In this day and age of technology so much can be found out about you, through your profiles and public posts, before your Ideal Client joins your community.   With this in mind the first thing I suggest you do is check your social media profiles, particularly on the platform(s) you are going to be using to connect with your Ideal Client.

What to check for:
o   Is your profile set to public view? You will be amazed what a difference it makes when getting exposure for your posts.
o   Does your profile make it really clear what you do to help your clients? For example, in the past, many years ago, I was a commercial buyer, but now I am an online business empowerment coach. I needed to update my profiles to reflect the change. Even if you are self-employed as a coach, you can still reflect that in your profiles.
o   Does your profile have links to your relevant Facebook and LinkedIn pages, groups etc? You can include your website too if you have one. A word of note here – it is not essential to have a website to get your

coaching business up and running. My approach is let's get the money coming in first and then invest when the business is in profit.

No matter where in the world you are based, networking online is a valid opportunity to share your message to a wider audience. There are specific on-line networking groups, or you can find groups that specifically focus on your Ideal Client's pain. The important thing is to become an active participant of the group so people get to know you. You can search for groups using your keywords. Once you have identified the Facebook groups you want to engage with, ask to join the group and set notifications to "see first", so you can nurture conversations in the group. Do not overwhelm yourself by seeking to join 20 groups. Be selective, similar to attending live networking groups. You do want to join groups where your Ideal Clients hang out though because that is the ultimate aim of networking - being in the proximity of others you can support and who can support you. They could be groups where your Ideal Client's symptoms are addressed, such as overwhelm, or where they are seeking advice for example, they cannot get pregnant.

Within your chosen groups respond to posts regularly and consistently. Share advice, offer opinions, suggest options. At this stage I would not try to sell your service or products; unless it is in response to a specific post inviting you to do so. The aim of engaging on the posts is to build a relationship with the community, sharing your knowledge and being supportive to others. This allows the community to get to know you, like you and trust you. And when they trust you, they will buy!

In amongst the five, or so, groups you have identified, try to pick a couple where promotion of freebies, links and programmes are allowed.

Remember, every opportunity is a marketing opportunity.

Within my own Facebook group, I invite the community to share links and services. It would be wonderful to welcome you in to the group - https://www.facebook.com/groups/StephanieThompsonGetFocusedFastAttractingClients

I regularly hear new coaches say they do not want to promote their services in other people's group. I appreciate this is down to fear of being visible, fear of overstepping the rules, lack of confidence, etc. What I say in response is "If you do not step out of the shadows then your Ideal Client cannot find you". Go back to your "big why" to remind yourself why you are setting up your coaching business. In the words of Tony Robbins – for every choice there is a consequence. In this instance if you choose not to engage and promote in other groups then the consequence is your Ideal Client will not know about you and therefore cannot purchase your products or services.

It is very easy to become a stalker on social media. This is where you stay quiet and see what everyone else is doing or saying; then the magical post comes where you can "share your freebie". You take a big breath and you share your link. Then you wait with bated breath for that first download. But nothing comes. You face your inner demons of "I'm not good enough", "nobody wants what I have to offer" and you go back to stalking, or worse still you throw it all up and stick with the very stressful 9-5 job!

I can assure you, right here, right now, "you ARE good enough"!

I can assure you "they absolutely DO want what you offer"!

The difficulty is - they don't know who you are. That magical "know, like and trust" has not been built and so they just scroll past.

Sorry, there is no magical formula for the wording to use! It is purely and simply "be visible consistently". Share what you are doing, share your knowledge, build relationships to create that "know, like and trust".

Also, being very realistic, the relationship doesn't build overnight. It builds over time, which I why you have to be consistently constant.

Remember, as a rough guide - a client is more likely to take action after they have seen your messages SEVENTEEN times. So, as well as posts, blogs, vlogs, newsletters, memes, Facebook Lives here are some other opportunities that may come your way to appear in front of your Ideal Client.

Be a guest Expert in another Facebook Group. Often, in other people's groups, you will see an appeal for Guest Experts. This is usually your opportunity to talk for up to an hour on your expert area.

Podcasts (audio) and Interviews (live). Much like the above, you will see appeals for hosts wanting speakers. Often with a podcast and interviews the host provides you with a list of questions prior so you can prepare your answers and, with the hosts encouragement, you can share the work you do and the benefits your clients achieve during your answers. In the name of reciprocity (I love that word), it is polite to invite the host to do similar in your Facebook Group. There is no time like the present, so start today building your connections with others. You are not pitching; you are not selling; you are sharing your knowledge sufficiently that they realise you know your stuff. Then when they want to know more about you, your social media profile is your business card. Effectively you are networking online, so put as much effort into it as you would when attending a live networking event.

Decide on your connection strategy in others' groups.
o   Are you going to interact with their posts?
o   Are you going to post questions?
o   Are you going to share information?
o   Are you going to engage in the group daily/weekly/monthly?

Decide what is going to be YOUR connection strategy, on YOUR OWN social media pages?
o   Are you going to post questions and seek their input? How often?
o   Are you going to post polls so you can gain information? How often?
o   Are you going to share a video every day/week/month? What are the topics?
o   Are you going to put a call-to-action on every single post?
o   Are you going to be your authentic self and share personal information about your life/family/friends/activities/etc.?

Something else to consider is how are you connecting with your Ideal Client? The main choices are:
o   Audio
o   Visual
o   Written
o   Imagery.   You may also be influenced by the platform you use, for example Instagram works with imagery very nicely.

Start off by working in a media you are comfortable with and then build up. Ideally you want to aim for working in video, or preferably live. The Facebook algorithm favours you speaking live and therefore your organic reach increases. Being live also builds that "know, like and trust" quicker too.

Wherever it is appropriate, add a call-to-action, even something as simple as "put an emoji in the comments for more information", which builds engagement. The readers that take the action are showing they have an interest in what you are talking about and so they come a step closer to being your warm audience.

You can share your story in various ways, in many places and in different formats - magazines, podcasts, live trainings, on stage, videos, YouTube and the list goes on. Try and think outside the box too, be creative. It is those that create intrigue, capture the reader/listener imagination who gain the interest.

Many years ago, I read a story about a university marketing graduate who wanted a job in a very elite company. First day, he sent a message to follow the instructions. Second day, he sent a small dish. Third day, a bottle of water. Fourth day, one of those things that looks like a piece of carboard, but when you add water, it expands into a sponge along with the instructions of what to do. Once the sponge expanded it had a message saying "you really need this innovative guy". He got the job!

Are you engaging with your client's imagination? Are you attracting their attention?

I mentioned earlier we have an attention span of 8-seconds on social media nowadays. So you need something that makes them stop, look AND want to know more. It can be graphics, music, photographs, even use of your brand colours. Something to capture their imagination and stop them scrolling so fast.

Finally, I want to talk about meditation. In the beginning I didn't have time for meditating. I found it irritating and my mind wandered to all the tasks I had to do. I thought it was a waste of time. However, I kept an open mind and eventually found something that really works for me. Sleep meditations. The one I like most is a 3-hour wealth and abundance meditation. Drifting off to sleep to that mesmeric voice is wonderful. I personally choose to listen to the same meditation each night, because I want to build the neural pathways in my brain, to strengthen them as much as possible. Listening to the same one every evening may not be for you and that is ok. You have to find something that works for you.

Oh and here is one final quick tip before we close this Chapter. I want to talk about re-purposing. Just because you have created a video does not mean that's the end of it. Many videos also create an audio file, which you can use. You can take sound bites and turn them into Twitter posts. You could take a still image and make a graphic for Instagram. You could even take the whole transcript and turn it into a blog.

As we draw to the end of stage three, hopefully, you have gained some insight on:
- o Giving your Ideal Client a personality.
- o The importance of being in flow
- o The magical words "so that"
- o Choosing stories that you are comfortable sharing
- o Speaking authentically to your client (even possibly using one of those voice-to-text apps to help).
- o Posts should cover why me, why this, why now.
- o Check your profile is up to date because it is your social media business card.
- o It is not beneficial to be a Facebook stalker.
- o Be consistently constant in your communications and building those relationships.
- o To be innovative and capture their imagination through your communications.

I would love to hear about your success, so please do drop me a note to stephanie@stephaniethompsoncoaching.com

Also, if you have any questions, please send them to the same email address above.

Chapter 5 –

How do clients know you are any good?

When you get right down to it, it's a chicken and egg situation really. It is necessary for clients to share how you helped them, so others will come. But you have to have clients, in the first place to be able to actually make that difference for them. So where do we start? Have you heard of the 3Rs?

I'm going to show my age now, because when I was young, they taught the 3Rs in school which were Reading, Writing and Arithmetic. I never really understood why the 3Rs when there was only one – Reading, but I think they were taking some poetic license on the sounds of the words. Anyway, I digress and we have only just started the Chapter! Let's get back on track.

The 3Rs – Reach, Revenue and Reputation and in this Chapter I am concentrating on Reputation.

How do we build our reputation?

When you first start-up in business, as a coach, you practice your skills on willing participants such as family, friends and possibly even friends of family and friends too. You are very studious to make sure you do everything right. You follow all the crib sheets, all the guidelines, apply all your learning and you achieve the results you have been learning to deliver. Success. Wooohooo. Absolutely fantastic. Now you, your training coach, family and friends all know how good you are.

So what happens next?

Do you write an advert and put it in the local post office or shop window and wait by the phone for people to call?

Do you spend hundreds, or even thousands, of pounds to create a website and wait for the emails to come pouring in?

Do you spend pounds and pounds on Facebook Ads and wait for the download clicks to start mounting up, as people join your mailing list?

Or do you do all of these and start your business with debt?

Well, I am here to tell you, you don't have to go into debt. You can grow organically with the support of testimonials.

Ask as many family and friends and friends of theirs if you can hold a session or two with them (or however many is appropriate to your skill). Don't ask for any money, although donations are always useful of course. This is your gift to them. There is a very slight catch though. In exchange you would like them to write you a testimonial. Nine times out of ten, people are very willing to help and support you in whatever way they can, in exchange for a free session, so take it from me, you will get testimonials from this activity.

"What about people I worked with months ago Stephanie? I helped them achieve fabulous transformations, but it was a long time ago......" I hear you say.

And this is exactly what happened to me initially too. I hadn't thought to ask for testimonials at the time, but now I needed them to be able to expand my business. So, I put my thinking-cap on, did a bit of research and came up with doing a survey. I sent the survey to ALL the people I had helped in the past. Now take it from me not everyone will respond, but you only need a few, so don't worry. When I did this activity, I sent out 29 questionnaires and received 5 in return. Five was enough and they were golden nuggets!

I sent out 9 questions, one of which asked if I could use their name, their town and country and a photograph of them too. A photo adds further credibility to the testimonial if you get their permission to use one.

If you do not have any previous clients then get to work with some friends and relations quickly. It is not about the money at this point, it is the testimonials you want.

Not sure what questions to ask? The trick is to plan forward so the answers you receive are useful. There are free versions of apps you can use to do a survey, often limiting you to 9 questions, so asking the usual questions like name, age, which town they live in, if they are married, wastes a lot of valuable opportunity to gather data for your testimonial. I am not saying my questions are perfect, so please feel free to amend, adapt, adopt or alter any that don't resonate with you. Here are the questions I sent out, as an example for you...

To find out how they felt before working with me I asked - What was going on in your life before working with me?

To find out how they felt after working with me - the transformation they experienced – I asked - How did your life change after having worked with me?

To find out what was their aha moment, I asked - What did you gain/what insight did you get from working with me?

Ideal Clients buy with their emotions, so to find out the emotions they felt working with me, I asked - How would you describe working with me? What did you like most?

We talk about using the same language as your Ideal Client, so they identify with you easier. So, I asked a question to understand the words they would use when talking about me to others. The question was - Please give 3 statements regarding the benefits of working with me.

It is always useful too if clients would recommend you, so I asked just that - Would you recommend me to others? If so, why?

It is good to get comments in the client's own words, so this is another question I asked - Please finish this sentence. "Working with Stephanie is ...."

I also made sure I asked a confirmation question to gain their official agreement, which was - May I use your responses in a testimonial for promotional purposes? If yes, may I include your name, city, country and a photo, together with your website or social media link. I will happily send the testimonial to you for approval before publishing. Please send your photo and links here –
stephanie@stephaniethompsoncoaching.com

And the final question gives them an option to say anything else that has not yet been covered in the survey - Please add any other comments you wish to make here.

Once I received their responses, making sure to do one at a time so I did not mix peoples answers up, I sat and created a testimonial paragraph using their replies. Then popped it on an email thanking them for replying and asking if they were happy with the following testimonial for me to use. Every one of them said yes, bless them and that is how I got started with my testimonials.

As I have gone on to work with more and more clients, I have made it a habit to ask for a testimonial when working with them. This way the testimonials I use in promotional material are relevant and fresh. Plus, as you become more confident in your skills your testimonials reflect the depth at which you can create those transformations for your clients.

The next question is, where to use the testimonials? Well, anywhere really! I definitely use them on my website, I put them in posts, I make them into graphics, I use them in blogs and newsletters. Wherever it is appropriate to the topic.

The client has very kindly given you permission to use their words (and hopefully their photograph too). Where I can, I share their website address too. It is only fair, being as they were so kind to provide me with a testimonial that I spread the love too.

Now let's move onto Social Proof.

And straight away I can hear you ask, "Stephanie, what is the difference between social proof and testimonials? They're the same, aren't they?" The straightforward answer is "Yes" and "No".

Testimonials can be received via social media. My tip here is to always take a screenshot. Out of curtesy, you can check with the author if it is ok to use their kind words elsewhere. Once received, you can do so, wherever is appropriate.

Social Proof are the comments, the engagement, the click "likes" and "loves" your posts, pages and groups receive. Social Proof is the organic confirmation of your skills and ability.

If you look on my Facebook Personal Profile you will see some posts have massive engagement, with loads of comments, loads of click "loves" and click "likes" and some have very little. It is the engagement on those posts that are your social proof.

To be honest, I don't do an awful lot on my personal profile, except for ..... wait for it ..... I am passionate about knitting. I know I am going back a while now but when I was first pregnant there was no such thing as a pregnancy test to buy over the counter. You went to the doctors, provided a sample, and the following week you returned to find out if you were pregnant or not.

I remember that day as clear as a bell. I walked down to the doctors and got the confirmation. As I was walking back, through the village, I called into the wool shop (it's not there anymore, it is an Indian restaurant now) where I purchased a pattern, knitting pins and some wool. I started knitting that night and have had a knitting project on the go ever since (except for a year, about 4 years ago, when I moved house and was renovating – there was far too much dust to be knitting at that time!). If I don't knit, I almost feel like I am getting withdrawal symptoms. It is a compulsion that I have to knit every day, even if only for half an hour. And since I picked up my pins again, about 4 years ago, I have got into the habit of putting a photograph up of each of my creations.

I was on a mission, just before the first covid lockdown, to knit and use up every piece of wool in the house so I was knitting stripy cardigans and all sorts to use the wool up. I was just getting to the last 2 balls of wool when I saw lockdown coming and virtually had a panic attack. What on earth was I going to do if I didn't have any wool???? So very quickly I dashed to the wool shop and purchase 5 balls of virtually every colour and I have been working my way through them ever since.

What I didn't think about though was the buttons needed to finish the garments!!!! So, at the time of writing this, although I have knitted three cardigans, they are all sitting waiting for buttons before I can give them to the recipients. I didn't quite think that bit through, did I? At least the wool lasted through the first lockdown! I can't wait to go wool shopping again! It is my guilty pleasure. I can spend hours in a wool shop!

Anyway, I digress again!!! What on earth did I start telling you that story for?

Oh yes. Getting social proof.

When I post the photographs of my knitting creations everyone absolutely loves them and I gain so much engagement you would not believe. Which is so lovely.

The downside is .... The engagement is not connected to sharing my career knowledge and skills.

The point I am making here is .... You need to have the right engagement for your social proof reputation to build. I have a great reputation for knitting cardigans! Hahahaha. Fortunately, my Facebook Group has lots and lots of activity and social proof, so that's a perfect balance if you ask me.

The other thing to think about with social proof and it is a fine line, so I will tell you first and then share what I do.

Facebook is a public forum and anyone can see the comments when it is a public post. If it is a private post then, of course, the reach is smaller. However, some people say ".... if it is on Facebook, you do not need to seek permission to use the comments elsewhere ...".

To be honest, so that it fits with my values and integrity, I will do a screenshot and message the sender, with a copy of the it asking for their permission to use as social proof or a testimonial. For me, it is better to be safe than sorry and I certainly don't want to alienate a potential client by abusing use of their kind words.

Do capture every kind word that is said on your profiles/posts. Build yourself a folder of testimonials and social proof. Support comes in many formats and this folder will help you when you are questioning your abilities, when you are wondering if you are good enough, when you are looking for support to carry on what you are doing. As well as be a resource for sharing your skills and ability of course.

In this Chapter, we are talking about .... How do clients know you are any good?

The answer is - By being visible. By sharing your knowledge. By being your authentic self. And one of the best ways to do this is by networking either in person at live events, or online. Shine your true, authentic self and people will come towards you, they will engage with you, they will ask questions, they will seek their own internal confirmations that they want to work with you.

As I have said previously in the book - there is no magical formula - it is purely and simply "be visible consistently". Share what you are doing, share your knowledge, build that "know, like and trust" and remember it takes time.

I am sure you have heard the saying "It takes a lifetime to build a reputation, it takes a moment to lose it!"

Building your reputation is not a tick in the box exercise, it is a constant activity throughout all your working life. Combine that with the fact that a client is more likely to take action after they have seen your messages approximately SEVENTEEN times, and your work is never done.

Raving fans are an essential part of building your reputation.

I was attending a business conference not so long ago and the event host asked everyone to sit down. Then he asked a few short questions ....

"Stand up if you build your business through advertising in newspapers and magazines". He then asked them to sit down.

"Stand up if you build your business through TV or radio advertising". Sit down.

"Stand up if you build your business through social media advertising". Sit down.

"Stand up if you build your business through word of mouth". Sit down.

The first 3 questions I would guestimate between 10 and 40% of the audience stood up. The final question referring to word of mouth, about 60% of the audience stood up! It was very very interesting to see that much of a difference between the different answers.

The reason I am sharing this is because your raving fans count for so much more. It is those raving fans that say "oh you want to talk with .... they will be able to help you with that". It is the raving fans that support you, provide the feedback when you ask, are a good sounding board if you want to gauge the audience, are a good source of testimonials etc.

And how do you get raving fans?

By you delivering what you say you'll deliver and exceeding their expectations. By under-promising and over-delivering. By supporting and encouraging them to grow, expand and achieve their dreams. By believing in them and their ability to achieve. Deliver that promised transformation, they will be your fans for life and shout your abilities from the roof tops.

If I go right back to the beginning of this Chapter, I talked about working with friends and family to gain those initial testimonials, so you can build your reputation. They are still your clients. Don't lose sight of any of your clients along the way. Just because they have worked with you once, does not mean they will not work with you again. They are your warm audience. They have already experienced what it is like to work with you. Obviously, if they decide to unsubscribe that is their choice. With the ones who remain, nurture them, care for them, share what is going on without being pushy. By remaining in their minds-eye, they will remember you and share your abilities in their conversations. All the nurturing is worth it; it counts to gaining a word-of-mouth reputation, the best form of reputation anyone can gain!

Another way of building your reputation is via your newsletters and blogs. Yes, there is a difference, so let's tackle newsletters first.

Newsletters are chatty, sharing the news, sharing what's happening with the business, maybe refers to articles you think your readers would be interested in, shares what is coming up, what events are going to be happening, how the preparations are going etc. They are like a mini-magazine with pictures and catchy headlines that the reader can dip in and out. A headline catches their eye so they read a bit more. You know the sort of thing.

Now blogs - they are a bit different. When I first encountered blogs, I thought they were like newsletters, but on one topic and really were thoughts and musings of the writer. Oh no. I have learned a lot since then. In particular, blogs tend to share really valuable information like ...
- o   10 steps to .....
- o   How I reclaim time in my day .....
- o   Does meditation have a place in business?

There is a purpose behind what is being said in each blog. It is sharing the writer's knowledge and expertise. Not thoughts and musings as I first thought! It is an article to capture the attention of potential clients and take them on a journey to an aha moment, to a discovery point, to a realisation point AND ...

And this is the crucial bit ...

There is a call-to-action! The purpose of a blog is for the reader to learn a bit and then take action. To discover more …. which might be to book a discovery call, or click through to download more information, or to book on to some free training.

Another valuable piece of information is to write blogs with Search Engine Optimisation (otherwise known as SEO) in mind. Often blogs are on the internet and can be searched by Google and the likes. So, if the blogs are optimised it is going to appear in the feed of those wanting to know more on the topic. Because they have searched for it.

These search results are another way of building your reputation. Ensuring your blogs are of value and a useful resource. You establish yourself as the "go to" expert for that topic. It makes for interesting pondering, doesn't it? I found it quite fascinating when I learned this.

And here is one final thing I want to share before we end this Chapter.

There are 4 things a business needs to be able to succeed:

1. The ability to generate and grow sales. Without clients and sales there is no business.

2. The ability to grow and expand the business. Now, don't get me wrong. I know not everyone wants to grow enough to take over the world, but no matter how big your dreams, do ensure your systems allow you the ability to expand sufficiently to accommodate that growth. Systems really do help to alleviate the amount of manual work you do in your business. If you would like to know more about this then please drop me an email to stephanie@stephaniethompsoncoaching.com

3. The ability to create more and more value for customers, so they keep returning. This is how you develop the raving fans I was talking about earlier. The key is to keep up-to-date with changes in your area of expertise, see what is trending, remain current for both new and raving fans. That's how popstars, like Sir Cliff Richard and Sir Tom Jones stay popular, because they adopt and adapt the trends to keep them current.

4. And finally, the ability to be perceived as an expert in your field. If you can niche in one area and be known as the expert, you will get

more invites to be a Guest Speaker, or podcast interviewee and your reputation will spread, which will ultimately result in clients seeking you out.

Oh and here is one final quick tip. When you receive a testimonial or a kind word share your enthusiasm with how you felt, create it into a story and post it. Share the love, it may just be enough to help a potential client become a paying client. You never know.

As we draw to the end of stage four, hopefully, you have gained some insight on:
- o Testimonials and social proof.
- o Building your reputation.
- o Nurturing your raving fans.
- o Newsletters.
- o Blogs.

I would love to hear about your success, so please do drop me a note to stephanie@stephaniethompsoncoaching.com

Also, if you have any questions, please send them to the same email address above.

Chapter 6 –

Is Branding Important?

By being consistent with your visual branding, across your communication channels, it builds a connection for your potential clients.

The logo alone is not your brand.

Your brand is the collection of stories, graphics and colours. The feelings and emotions they evoke. Taken together as a whole, they enable your potential client to make a decision … to invest …. with you.

This ensemble of colours, images, fonts, evoked emotions and feelings enables people to notice what you are about. It gives them a preview of you before they meet with you virtually or in person. Once they meet you, they get to know more about your uniqueness and that magical "know, like and eventually trust" builds. Impressions really do count.

This Chapter is all about your brand avatar. We have an Ideal Client Avatar; well, we have a brand avatar too. I will be honest, it is only when I completed my Brand Avatar work that my Ideal Client really took shape. So, if you are struggling to identify your Ideal Client, do complete these exercises in this Chapter. It was a real aha moment for me.

To be totally open and transparent I want to take this moment to acknowledge Emily Roach-Griffin of Biz BFF. I love Emily's approach to identifying your Brand Avatar, it's the best one I have ever come across. This is her exercise to create a brand board - the document that holds key pieces of information you will refer to time and time again. Plus, it will be really useful when you are engaging a web designer too.

What is your brand avatar? It is what, or who, brings your brand to life for you, so you know why you are using that image, or this photograph, or those colours. Let me take you through a few questions and I have also made a couple of suggested answers to get you started. I am sure there are many more options, so let your creativity flow and have some fun.

o If your brand was a person, what are their characteristics? Friendly?
   Quirky? Sophisticated? Bold? Girl next door?
   My brand person is warm and friendly, welcoming and down to earth,
   always smiling with positive energy. They are quietly confident with
   a strong focus, who makes things happen.

o If your brand avatar was to wear clothes, what would they wear?
   Jeans and t-shirt, suit and blouse? Ball gown? Sports wear?
   Mine wears a jacket, t-shirt, jeans and loafers. She has that air of
   casual confidence and enjoyment of life.

o If your brand avatar was going to decorate their house, what would it
   look like? Minimalist? Bohemian? Rustic? Coastal?
   For my brand avatar – their house is minimalist, clean lines, lots of
   white everywhere.

o Describe their favourite room, in their house. Vibrant? Elegant?
   Nautical? Chintz? Luxurious?
   For me it is all about the lounge, or the kitchen, being chic, feminine,
   luxurious and warm.

o Where does your brand avatar hang out? With family and friends?
   Small groups? Large groups? Loud, noisy with lots of music? Small,
   intimate, lots of laughter? Sophisticated, elegant with quiet
   conversation?
   My brand avatar goes out for dinner with several people all sat
   around, in a relaxed atmosphere, where they are laughing, having
   fun, with lots of camaraderie, interesting conversations, support and
   caring.

Do you know something? I really love doing this piece of work. I find it a
lot of fun and I love getting into the psyche of my brand avatar and
bringing it to life. Branding is little to do with colours or images, more to
do with the feelings and emotions you build within your business.

On another level, it is also bringing my Ideal Client avatar to life too.

o What does your brand avatar do for fun or relaxation? Walking?
   Knitting? Ski-ing? White water rafting? Baking? Fishing? Gardening?
   Well, if you've picked up nothing else about relaxation, you will know
   that I absolutely adore knitting and so, of course, my brand avatar
   relaxes by knitting.

This exercise is building up into an image, a picture of what your brand stands for, even what your Ideal Client stands for too. With my examples so far, I have a picture of joy, laughter, support, confidence, relaxed, clean and simple, nothing fluffy.

What image have you got so far for your brand avatar and Ideal Client avatar?

- How do people feel when they are with your brand avatar? Do they feel relaxed? Invigorated? Comfortable? Energised? Focused?
  I would like to think that my brand avatar is the comfortable, girl next door, who is capable, engaging and takes action; that the people around her also feel comfortable, safe, able to ask anything; they feel energised and focused.

- Which actor, character, style icon would represent your brand avatar? James Bond? Lara Croft? Dame Judy Dench? Jude Law? Jennifer Anniston? Karren Brady? Anita Roddick?
  I had to think long and hard on this one and I came up with a couple of names … Holly Willoughby, Doris Day and Fern Britton. I finally settled on Fern Britton

Potential clients, in the first instance, are attracted to the look of your brand, just like shopping on the high street. Some shops you just don't fancy visiting. Others you can spend hours in. Your Facebook Page is your shop window, before they enter your community, usually on your Facebook Group. What does your page say about you? I am sure you have walked past many shop windows in your time and thought "ooooo I think I'll pop in here and see what else it has to offer". The shop window attracts you in, in the first place. This is the job of your Facebook Business Page, or social media platform profiles, which has been mentioned in a previous Chapter.

If there was just a coloured door into a shop and nothing else, would you go in? You might be looking for a pair of spectacles and end up in a pet-food shop! The shop window is an important part of attracting your clients - the style, the imagery, the colour. I am sure you have scrolled through Facebook and seen various pages that just do not appeal and others that really jump out to you. Everyone sees things differently, so there is no right or wrong here. It's all about being consistent in your online presence and creating a connection with your potential clients. Plus, being your authentic self no matter what. If you are a colourful character in life, then be a colourful character on your communication channels. Be true to you.

Think of your Facebook Page, your shop window, as a first date. What outfit are you going to wear on your first date? What is your brand style? If you are all about the comfort, you are not going to put on 6-inch stiletto heels for your first date, are you? Well, hopefully not! You want your clients to identify with you and 'want to get to know you more' by coming on the page and seeing what you have to say.

- o What is your Brand Avatar's favourite colours? I absolutely adore wearing powder blue, mauve, pink and turquoise, along with navy blue as a staple colour. Guess what my brand colours are?

- o What is your Brand Avatar's favourite pattern? Geometrics? Stars? Spots? Leopard print? Swirls? Block colour?
  For me it is stars! My love of stars has spanned many years. In fact, when I was asked what my group name would be, when I started teaching the Energy Alignment Method to my first group I said "Constellation". My reason? Because everyone in my group is a star! And together they are a Constellation. I love stars, you will often hear me say "you are a star" too.

Have you got a feel for what and who your Brand Avatar is? Could you create a mood board for your brand now?

Here's something you might like to try now you have got these answers so far …

- o Pop onto Pinterest and start searching images available for the words you have written down. See what comes up and collect the images you like into a Pinterest board of your own. You can build it up bit by bit, or you can spend a day having fun and choosing. I've got to admit I could spend hours doing this, so if you are short of time make sure you set an alarm!!!! When you have finished, what you will end up with is a collection of images that represents your brand.

- o The next phase is to start narrowing down those images. There will be some images, styles, colours that jar against the rest, so delete them straight away. Then look at the remaining images and select the ones that make you feel how you want your clients to feel when they interact with your brand. Are you starting to really feel into your brand now? I know I did when I did this exercise.

o Now you have got the images of your brand, let's start working on the words. This is where journaling can help. Here are some questions you can journal against to see what comes out .....

o How do you want your client to feel when they work or interact with your brand?
I want my client to feel loved and cared for. To feel important, believed, trusted and understood. I want my Ideal Client to feel clear on their intention, safe and heard. That they can ask anything. They have fun. They feel empowered, capable and excited for what is happening now and in the future.

o What strengths and personality traits do you have that help your customers feel that way?
Based on how I would like them to feel from the earlier questions, my own personality traits and strengths I bring are my patience, how I love sharing my knowledge, my energy, positivity, enthusiasm and my ability to laugh.

o What elements from your own personal style are important to bring into your branding?
I like to bring confidence, elegance, love, joy, fun and laughter to my clients through my brand and through my programmes. Along with my organisational skills and my ability to see the big picture, as well as be able to work in the detail too.

Once you have identified some key words, highlight the one that really resonate with you – and there is no limit to how many you pick. Take one of those words, any one that you have highlighted, place it in the centre of a mind-map and capture all the things that help you to create that emotion; that feeling. I shared earlier in the book how to do a mind-map. Then it is back to Pinterest to capture images that portray your chosen key emotions.

Can you see how you are really getting into the psyche of your brand, and at the same time really getting into the psyche of your Ideal Client avatar too?

Now we are going to bring all this information together into some key images that inspire you, are cohesive to your vision and give you the overall feel of your business. This is where the hard work starts – because it is a case of reviewing all those fabulous images you selected on Pinterest and narrowing them down. You can delete the images that don't resonate straight away. Choose key images that really mean something to you and your business; that portrays how you want your client to feel when they are with you. And I don't just mean physically, or on screen, I mean when they are looking at your shop window (your Facebook Page), when they open your emails, when they read your newsletters or blogs, when they engage on any of your social media platforms.

Your brand board is effectively a selection of words and images, colours, fonts, all on one sheet so you have the information to hand and can share quickly and easily with your design team.

This is what a brand board would include:

Eight images that truly portray how you want your client to feel when they come into your arena. I also jot the description under each image, so I am reminded what it represents.
   o I have an image of ladies gathered round a computer with the words "Community – focused and supported".
   o Another image is mugs of hot chocolate in front of a log fire with the words "Atmosphere – relaxed, loved and cared for".
   o Then I have an image of sparkles with hues of blue, pink and purple. The words are "Emotion – excited about what to open next".
   o There is a picture of a lady laying on a sofa with her dog, relaxing. My description says "Ultimate Aim – stress free lifestyle".
   o There is an image of a lovely lady smiling, whilst outdoors. The words are "doing it in style – girl next door".
   o Oh, I love this one – it is a picture of piles of coins with seedlings growing on the top. I describe this as "sow the seeds and nurture them".
   o Then it comes to a picture of a room. It is very white, very tidy but with lots going on. My words are "clean, simple and organised".
   o The final image is of ladies sat around a table eating and laughing, which, for me, portrays "Atmosphere – relaxed, fun and laughter".

As I step back and look at these 8 images – they all represent how I want clients and potential clients to feel when they are engaging on my social media pages, reading my emails, getting to meet with me physically or virtually.

Don't worry, it doesn't always come together perfectly first time. Print your images out, put them up on the wall and live with them for a few days. Does the collection, overall, give you the feeling you want your clients to feel when engaging with you? You may need to tweak until you get that exact feeling you are looking for. In fact, when friends come round, particularly someone who would be your Ideal Client, if they weren't your friend, ask them what they feel when looking at your gallery of images.

Ideally on your Brand-Board you would have four to six colours in your colour palette. These would include your logo, text and highlight colours. Make sure you include both their hex and RGB codes, so you can have consistency in all you create.

I represent these colours on my brand board by having circles of colour with the code's underneath. I have 6 in total. My 3 main colours, my text colour, the back ground colour if I cannot have white (which is my personal preference) and an accent colour. The accent colour doesn't always get used, but if I am short of one more then this is the one I will use.

If you want some ideas for layout of brand boards then have a look on Pinterest, searching for brand board and see what comes up. You can also do the same for colour palettes to help chose complimentary colours and identify their hex and RGB codes.

If you want to dig deeper into colours then you can do some research on the psychology of colour. What I will say at this point is, it is very easy to run down rabbit holes doing this sort of thing. It is a great excuse to procrastinate on moving your business forward. Let's just get your business flourishing and as automated as possible – then you can start tweaking when you have more time (whilst earning).

When I review the colours I have in my brand, together with the words from the exercises we have done so far, I am rather pleased with the outcome.

My colours and their meaning are:
- o Pink – warmth, nurture, calm, respect and love
- o Blue – determination, self-sufficient, ambition
- o Mauve – stimulation, individual, wealth
- o Navy – trust, loyal, sincere, success

For me, I think they are a great balance for what I want to portray to my clients!

Another image to include on your Brand-Board is an image of your logo, your social media icon and also your favicon (if you have a website). What is the difference I hear you ask?

- o The main image – usually your main logo.
- o The second image – usually for social media. Often a simpler icon than the main one. For example, the imagery without wording.
- o The third image is the favicon. What is a Favicon? Have a look on your bookmarks and you will often see a symbol (representative of the company) and the name. That symbol is called the Favicon.

And now we come to fonts. And this is a whole different ball game.

When I very first created my website, I was soooooooo thrilled with it. There was this gorgeous script font, all fancy and swirly and I looooooooved it. I spent hours and hours and hours creating my website and eventually published it. I was delighted.

Then, in one of the groups I am in, we were being asked what were our wins and I said that I had finally published my website. The lead of the group suggested I put it into the group and ask for feedback, which I did.

And the main feedback? They could not read the swirly font on their phone!

I was absolutely gutted.

I let it ride for a while, but then I scheduled some time into my diary and re-vamped my website.

You see I had created my brand board by then. I had also learnt so much from creating my website the first-time round. There were things I wanted to delete, others I wanted to add, colours I wanted to change and, of course, to change the swirly font. I will admit I did keep the stars though.

And do you know what? I adore my website now. I open it and feel so delighted with it. Yes, there are still things I would like to tweak, but overall, I love it! I accept it is very pink and it may change in the future. In fact, go and have a look and let me know what you think, there's lots to find out about me, like did you know I have climbed a 50-foot pole and jumped off the top of it? That was quite an experience! Anyway, have a look at my website and let me know what you think

I digress, as usual, let's get back on track – fonts and size.

Ideally you want three sizes – Headings – Subheadings - Copy or main text.

I have settled on two different but complementary fonts. One for Headings. The other for subheadings and main text.

Something to consider at this point, not all fonts are available everywhere, so do consider the systems you are using and have a look what is available. Sometimes you can download a font. I have found www.fontsquirrel.com is a good resource. Researching paired fonts is useful, so they are complimentary to each other and pleasing to the eye.

My favourite fonts are Raleway and Montserrat, followed by Verdana and then good old-fashioned Arial if all else fails. Not a swirly font in sight! If you like swirly fonts then the tip is to make sure there is wide spacing between the letters so it is easier to read. Majority of people, now-a-days, do everything on their mobile phone (despite its lack of functionality), so if your text is small, on the phone it is even smaller. If your text is swirly, on the phone it is difficult to read. These are all things to take into account when you are putting your fonts together. You don't want to lose potential clients before they even join you, because they cannot read what you are saying.

And now we come to the crux of it all. Key words. Or SEO by another name. Search Engine Optimisation!

As you have worked your way through the various Chapters, words will have cropped up often. Words to describe your brand. Words to describe your Ideal Client, their hell and their heaven.   We even worked on your message using "so that". All of this information now comes into the keywords section of your brand-board. Well! Not ALL of them! The key ones … that is why they are called your key words!!!! You can also use them as hashtags too.

What are the key words your Ideal Client will identify with, a lot? These are the words to include on your brand board.
- o Who they are – your niche, how they identify with you.
- o How they are feeling now – their hell.
- o How they want to feel – their heaven.

o What you are offering.

Everything I have mentioned so far – the eight pictures, the fonts, the brand colours, the three logos – they all fit onto one page-at-a-glance. It is all succinct and right in front of your eyes, so you are consistent wherever you have your brand. My sheet sits on my kitchen wall so I have the information available instantly – especially when I am being creative.

On the second sheet of my brand board I have the following:

My niche: I work with heart-centred life coaches ready to move into group work and not sure where to start or how to organise, structure and automate their business.

Key statements to support my niche to apply in the appropriate communication whilst maintaining consistency in my messaging include:
   o I help new life coaches who have their coaching skills and get great results working with their family and friends. Now they want to get paid for their skills but are overwhelmed by the information available and no idea where to start attracting paying clients.
   o I remove the overwhelm by showing life coaches how to get focused fast. I provide step-by-step detailed Masterclasses on how to get visible and focused fast on attracting clients. I help them walk towards their dream.
   o I help life coaches create a pathway to success for their clients and a pathway for prosperity for their business.
   o I help busy life coaches reclaim time in their day, instead of trying to build their business in the last hour of the day, when all they want to do is crash out on the sofa. I help them have the freedom of choice.
   o I help life coaches launch their programmes with confidence by conquering their negative inner voice, aligning their energy, the energy of their work environment and their business energy too. When everything is aligned and in flow attracting clients is so much easier.

My main links for my calls to action, for example
   o Website
   o Facebook Page
   o Facebook Group
   o LinkedIn Profile
   o Coffee and chat calendar link
   o Instagram link   etc., etc.

My brand values. The values that I live by and operate my business by.
- o Courage – courage to take action. If we don't grow, we die, and I want everyone to grow to their full and fabulous potential.
- o Clarity – clear, simple, easy-to-follow steps. Let's focus, keep it simple and make progress.
- o Connection – connection with our business and our clients. We are a unit and support each other.
- o Confidence – confidence in yourself and in your business

And lastly, **my guiding mantra**. This is the affirmation I say to myself every day before I start work and when things aren't going quite according to plan; when I am in need of a pep-talk. If you don't believe in yourself then why would your clients? So, make your affirmation big, and bold. Don't worry what other people will think; this is meaningful to you and motivates you! Use the words that resonate with you and help you stand in your power. My guiding mantra is ...

I am phenomenal,
I can do anything I want,
I listen to my instinct and act on it,
I achieve my goals with ease,
all that I need is within me now.

Your biography is also part of your branding. You would be amazed at the different requirements depending on who is requesting the biography. Short versions, long version, third person, first person. However, if you have a collection of information, in one place, where you can select what you want to say it saves you having to start thinking what to put and you can tailor it to the receiving audience. As you and your business evolve, then make sure you capture it in your biography so you don't lose sight of your journey too. Here is mine as it stands today ...

Stephanie Thompson, the Ready-to-Launch Mentor, is a multi-award winning, international online-business growth expert, number one international best-selling author and international radio presenter of "Stephanie's Business Coaching Show".
Having committed her working life supporting small, medium and global enterprises, plus owning three profitable companies herself, Stephanie brings a unique combination of heart-centred coaching, mentoring and accountability to her life coaching clients.
The Ready-to-Launch Academy trains hundreds of life coaches every year to plan, create and launch their online programmes in 90 days or

less; enabling the courage to take action, confidence in their programmes and connection to their first 10 clients.

Your photographs are the final sheet of the brand board. Some of mine are professionally done, others are really good photos, that I love, taken by friends and family. One thing I will say, especially if you squirm at the thought of using a photograph – it is a good way to build familiarity and rapport. Every engagement contributes to building the relationship with your potential clients. People buy from people they know, so being recognised (using photographs) is a great way to achieve this.

Here's one final quick tip …

Business Name – don't be too creative or too clever with your description. For example, if your business name is "jump4joy". When your Ideal Client is searching will they write "jump for joy", or "jump4joy"? Think about what your Ideal Client is going to type into the search bar. Usually, it is because they are in their hell state and looking for an answer. What would they type? This may give a clue as to what to call your business or social media group.

I am sure you will have picked up over time there are some people who are known by their name, whereas for others it is their business name. What do you want to be known by? You could retain your name and pivot your business from coaching to business coaching for example, but if your business is "In My Lounge Coaching" and you become a business coach who only engages on stage, then you would have to start setting everything up again. Think of the longevity of the name.

These are just some things for you to think about.

As we draw to the end of stage five, hopefully, you have gained some insight on:
- o Why branding is important
- o Your biography
- o Your business name.

I would love to hear about your success, so please do drop me a note to stephanie@stephaniethompsoncoaching.com

Also, if you have any questions, please send them to the same email address above.

Chapter 7 –

What programmes to offer?

There are some coaching programmes that are exact in their teaching. However, they do not allow for flexibility to tailor the programme specifically to your client's needs.

Marketing books ask "what is your USP?". What is your Unique Selling Point? And this is the area I am going to share in this Chapter. What makes you sooooo unique that clients come to you specifically,

OK, let's start with a picture of how everything fits together …..
- o Grab hold of a sheet of paper and a pen.
- o Top right-hand corner write HELL and top left-hand corner write HEAVEN, draw an arrow between the two and write Ideal Client Avatar along the line.
- o Below Heaven write OUTCOME.
- o To the left of OUTCOME write PROGRAMME
- o To the left of PROGRAMME write Low-Cost, or free, Valuable Offer.
- o To the left of Low-Cost, or free, Valuable Offer write FREEBIE (which should now be under HELL).

Brilliant. You now know what programmes to offer. Voila!!!!!

Hmmmmmm that's a bit of a short Chapter, isn't it? Hahahaha

Perhaps you would like some more details to understand what the picture is showing you? Yes? OK, let's go into some more depth and see if I can make this picture come alive for you ……

Start with your Ideal Client. Unless you know what your Ideal Client needs, then you can't deliver it. I covered Ideal Client, their hell and their heaven in an earlier Chapter. I do this work myself every 6-months, or so, both to remind me and also to allow my Ideal Client to evolve as I evolve. It is not a "job done – tick" task and then move on. This is a key part of your business foundations. Your Ideal Client is someone who you are going to talk to consistently, with passion. You want to help them; you want to serve them.

Having completed the Ideal Client Avatar work in an earlier Chapter, you now have all the information for both top corners of the diagram. What they are currently feeling, thinking, experiencing - their hell. You also know where they want to be, what they want to feel, what they want to have, to experience, to enjoy - their heaven. Their heaven state is also the outcome of your programme. The outcome is where they want to be!

So you now have information for the hell, the heaven and the outcome

OK, what next? The programme section.....

You know how your client wants to feel, when they come "out the other side". My question to you is, what are the tools and techniques, experience and knowledge you have, to bring about that desired outcome?

It is at this point that I am going to ask you to stop and think ...

Do not put EVERYTHING you know into the programme ...

I totally accept you are more than qualified in teaching a whole host of skills, for example, reiki, yoga, meditation, visualisation, business strategy, NLP, tapping, marketing, sales, finances, systems, various coaching qualification tools and techniques and the list may go on. HOWEVER, by throwing everything you know into the programme will not necessarily help your client.

I want you to take a moment. Take a deep breath. Still yourself. And listen. Inside. To your heart.

Looking back over your journey, what were the key things that really helped you? Thinking of where you started and where you are today you will have tried a number of different things. Which were the key things, that really worked? The ones that gave you those aha moments, when inspiration struck, when everything made sense for you?

Jot down the key learnings and the tools used to enable those key learnings on your page for the Programme section.

Now you have the beginning of your programme! It may just be a list, but it is the beginning.

Please, please, PLEASE, do NOT begin to develop the programme. I know it is really tempting, but all you need at this point is an outline. Trust me.

The last thing you want to do is spend weeks creating your course, the workbooks, the videos, the resources etc and then when it comes to the crux no-one buys it.

All you actually need, at this time, is the outline. Here are the key questions you want to answer:
- o What are the problems they are facing? Their hell.
- o What do they think they want? Their heaven.
- o Where are they now? What if they don't change?

These questions will have been answered within the Ideal Client work, so skip back, grab the information and put it here.
- o What is their actual need that you are addressing? For example, they may want a new partner, but they need to love themselves first before others can love them.
- o What is the benefit of completing the course. for the client? What's the deliverable? What will they achieve from attending this programme?
- o What on-going support are you offering, if any?
- o What is the name of the programme?
- o When are you delivering the programme?
- o How long will the programme last?
- o What is the format? For example is it in person, on-line, via zoom, via a Facebook live?
- o What do the clients need in place before starting, if anything? Maybe they need a certain qualification, or certain equipment to get full benefit.
- o What are you offering to the client following completion of the programme? For example, an opportunity to join a membership, or a Facebook community, or progress to the next level the programme/ qualification.
- o What is the investment - the fee they will pay?
- o How will you collect payment? For example via Paypal, Stripe, Bank Transfer.
- o What resources do you need to be able to deliver this programme? You only need a list at this point. Don't purchase until you know you have made a sale, otherwise it may be a false investment.

o What is the content of the programme? It may only be a few short paragraphs per teaching session, but it will remind you what you plan to do in each section, so when you come to develop and create the material you are consistent.

This is a standard set of questions I use regardless of which level of programme I am offering to my Ideal Clients.

Returning to the diagram you drew at the beginning of this Chapter, we have now completed the hell, the heaven. the outcome and now we have an outline of the programme.

You are making great progress.

Now we turn to the Low-Cost, or free, Valuable Offer section, which is often in the format of a live Challenge. It can be a 1, 3, 5, 10-day event, whatever is appropriate for your audience, your business and your offer. However, the format of this event is essential for two reasons.

1). Your Low-Cost, or free, Valuable Offer, is to help potential clients see their situation from a different angle and to realise there are solutions available. Doing the activities is going to interrupt their pattern; to help them achieve an aha moment or a transformation; where they will understand you can help them. The Low-Cost, or free, Valuable Offer is exactly what it says … of value to your potential clients and it is either low-cost or free - it is your choice. The important thing is to ensure this event shares activities that will improve their current situation. Plus, you also show them other activities can bring even greater transformations, but this is via your paid offer.

2). The other aim of this Low-Cost, or free, Valuable Offer event is to build "know, like and trust" with your potential clients to the point where they want to purchase from you. Seeing you and interacting with you is the quickest way to build rapport, because every engagement, prior to this point could, quite probably, have been only on-line. People buy from people they know. So doing this event is a great way for your Ideal Client to get to know you.

Are you wondering what the content of the event should be? The first thing to consider is what is your programme about. Your low-cost, or free, valuable offer should be a lead, into that programme.

Remember me telling you the story of the Solicitor and using a meditation as his lead-magnet? He made no sales because there was no connection from his freebie into his course. To avoid making this mistake please consider the connections between your PDF freebie, your Low-Cost, or free, Valuable Offer, your programme and the outcome you are trying to achieve for your Ideal Client. They should all be joined up and seamlessly move from one to the other, so your client can go on that journey to achieve their desired outcome!

Also, remember you are familiar with what you do and teach, so you may not always realise the value in what you consider to be a normal way of working or thinking. Not everyone thinks that way. The knowledge you are sharing in the Low-Cost, or free, Valuable Offer is very valuable, hence the name.

I shared with you previously I worked in the corporate world for 17 years. I was having a conversation with an old colleague a few months ago, where he was querying my Low-Cost, or free, Valuable Offer, what it was, what it included. My conversation with him, was very similar to what I am sharing with you now. The response I got, after I had finished talking was …. "but I do that every day"! It was at this point I was able to explain ….. yes, it is a normal way of working, in our particular company. However, not everyone has had the privilege of working there and so does not have the knowledge which will be of great value to them to learn. The moral of this story is do not underestimate your knowledge and what you think is everyday stuff. There are others who would value it very highly.

Use the same programme outline questions, mentioned earlier in this Chapter, to determine the details of your valuable free offer.

Returning to the diagram we have now completed the hell, the heaven and the outcome; we have an outline for the programme and we now have an outline of the low-cost, or free, valuable offer.

Next is your freebie, which just happens to be underneath the hell on the diagram. I appreciate the freebie is the starting point for your client's journey. However, to ensure everything is joined up, it is good to do the paper exercise I have just taken you through first.

There are two points of information to consider here …

1). What is your client experiencing at this moment in time? What solution can you offer them, that will make a big difference for them?

2). What is your Low-Cost, or free, Valuable Offer (the next stage in the process), or if you are skipping that part, the programme?

There definitely needs to be a seamless journey for the client to get from their hell state to their heaven state.

Your freebie can be in many formats, although it is usually a free, electronic, download e.g. a PDF. Here are some suggestions:
- o   Top 10 tips to ......
- o   5 steps to ......
- o   How to avoid these mistakes .....
- o   When to use ......
- o   Planner for ...
- o   Alternative suggestions to .....

One final thing I want to share with you before we close the Chapter – a confused person never buys. Remember my Four Ones? One Client. One Message. One Platform. One Call-to-action. No matter the chosen format to deliver your freebie and your Low-Cost, or free, Valuable Offer, always, always, always make sure you add a call-to-action at the end. Only one. If you offer too many options, they will not take action.

Here are some 'call-to-action' options ...
- o   "Put an emoji in the comments and I will send you details",
- o   "PM your email address and I will send you details",
- o   "Click this link for my download",
- o   "Click this button to secure time in my diary for us to chat", etc.

Just to re-iterate - only choose one call-to-action and make it as simple and straightforward for the client to complete as possible. Remember, an attention span of just 8 seconds is usual now-a-days, make the process complicated and you may lose the sign-up/sale.

As we draw to the end of stage six, hopefully, you have gained some insight on:

- o   What programmes to offer and how they join up.

I would love to hear about your success, so please do drop me a note to stephanie@stephaniethompsoncoaching.com

Also, if you have any questions, please send them to the same email address above.

SUCCESS begins at the edge of
your comfort zone.

What are you going to do today
that will push you further and
grow you faster?

Chapter 8 –

Investment made by the client into your programmes

The value comes from fully understanding your Ideal Client's current hell and what they will give to achieve their desired outcome. Value is in the eyes of the one paying the funds.

Let me say, right at the start of the Chapter - it is not how much your fee is but rather "what is the value, to your client, of achieving the results your programme delivers?".

If they are lying awake at night, worrying about how they are going to achieve certain things, and you have the solution that will take away those worries, then your solution is priceless to them. The trick comes in articulating the results you deliver, through your actions, your achievements, your testimonials and your marketing material! When your promotional material is clear and concise on the RESULTS your clients will achieve, when they invest funds with you, you will sell your programme time and time again.

Let's be absolutely clear here – your programme, alongside your client taking aligned action of course, must be able to deliver those results time and time again, not just claim to do so. Otherwise, credibility is lost, raving fans are not formed and your business is unable to progress, grow and expand.

When you appreciate the mindset that everything you post, email, blog etc., is a marketing opportunity then you are getting on the right track. Whether you are sharing something about your own story, talking about who you work with, share details of what clients have said about working with you, or even talking about your programmes everything is a marketing opportunity. Be it direct marketing - talking about your offer with a specific call-to-action. Or sowing the seeds, for example, who you work with, with no call-to-action. Every word you write or say is something to attract your Ideal Client's attention in one form or another.

Be clear in your communication, which comes from planning what you are saying in that particular editorial. There are 2 focuses of marketing:

- o Your potential client - Their desires, their dreams. The obstacles they want to overcome. Really talking to their heart and showing them things can change.

- o You (where you are building that "know, like and trust") - Talking about your philosophies, your beliefs, your own journey. Sharing your offer and the value of that offer (in other words what past and current clients say about working with you). Being their leader and showing them the way (because you have travelled that same path yourself). Sharing your story, so they can identify with you.

A huge tip here - never ever assume anything. Potential clients may not realise they are your Ideal Clients. They may not realise that a coach can help them overcome their situation. They may just think that "this is life, this is how it is for everyone".

This is why it is so important to talk about your story and how you went from your own "hell to heaven" so they can identify with you and realise that "life does not have to be like that". Those potential clients may not realise a coach can help them. It is up to you, through your marketing, to help people realise there are alternatives.

And believe in yourself! If you don't believe in yourself, in your programmes and how you can help others then how can a client believe in you? There is no such thing as "I am just a coach". By saying this, you are dismissing your value!

I have a daily mantra sitting on my shower door, so I see it every day .....

I am phenomenal,
I can do anything I want,
I listen to my instinct and act on it,
I achieve my goals with ease,
all that I need is within me now.

I know it sounds big headed, but there is only me that sees it. It helps me get into a positive mindset every day, it helps me believe in myself and what I do, it motivates me to keep doing what I am doing, knowing it is the right thing to do.

If someone was to use this as their message ......
"I have a programme that is going to make a difference, please buy it for £2500"

Or if I share my own message, which is effectively a landing/sales page ...

Are you lost on how to structure your coaching business to achieve prosperity and freedom?
Are you lacking a clear pathway to success for your clients and your business?
Has your business morphed and behind the scenes is chaotic?

It doesn't have to be this way!

If you are looking for a clear simple process to follow then "Plan Your Prosperous Coaching Business – a personalised plan, tailored to your offer", is for you. This programme, alongside regular one-to-one support and accountability, will help plan, structure, organise, and where possible automate, your coaching business. The resulting bespoke plan will reveal your pathway to creating success, prosperity and freedom.

The 90-day "Plan Your Prosperous Coaching Business" programme includes:
Initial jump-start call with Stephanie, where we dive deep into your business pathway and structure.
6 x Bi-weekly private online 1-1 calls for accountability, support and guidance.
6 x bi-weekly online group Q&A calls, with opportunity to collaborate.
Members only Facebook Messenger group.
Community support, inspiration and motivation in the well-established Facebook Group –
https://www.facebook.com/groups/StephanieThompsonGetFocusedFastAttractingClients
24/7 access to the Get Focused Academy.
Supported with how-to videos, workbooks, templates, worksheets and more.
Automating as much as possible to create more freedom.

What is it like to work with Stephanie?
"Just what I needed to get started on getting my program out to the world. Laid out in concise simple steps, no fluff or beating about the bush, and Stephanie's warm delivery made it easily digestible. I feel really confident now that I have a clear structure to get me working towards my

business goals. Thank you, Stephanie, you are awesome!" Elaine Wright, Italy – Unfrazzled and Unstuck.

If you would like to know more, please contact me: stephanie@stephaniethompsoncoaching.com

Of the two above - which one are you more likely to want to find out more about?

The latter one? Right? There is information, there is conviction, there is talk of where the client is now and where the client wants to be. The message is clear as to what they will get and one simple call-to-action too.

People buy with their hearts and then justify it with their heads. Don't focus just on the features of your offer; share what the benefit is of participating in your programme. The client wants to know "WIIFM", otherwise known as "What's In It For Me"?

Remember my first example - "I have a programme that is going to make a difference, please buy it for £2500"? Is this marketing post giving the client confidence they will get a return on their investment? What is in it for them - "... going to make a difference ..." but in what way? How? How long will it take? What do they have to do?

What does your own marketing message say?

Let's get back to having a positive mindset ... If you don't believe in yourself then how can clients believe in you?

Please, please, please do not allow yourself to think "They already know this" or "who am I to show them xyz?" You are doing your clients a total dis-service by not sharing your message.

All those clients out there who are suffering .... You DO have their answer!

Believe in yourself!
Believe in your programme.
Believe in your ability to make the difference for your client.

Although I am a business coach, I also have a spiritual side using the Energy Alignment Method to align energy and release negative energies. The Law of Attraction is very powerful. The Law of Vibration even more so. By improving our alignment with the Law of Vibration and therefore lifting our vibration it enables the Law of Attraction to manifest for us more easily. This is all connected to having a positive mindset and it really does work for …

- o Seeing the positive in things, relationships and situations
- o Being grateful for the love, joy and laughter in our lives as well as the materialistic things.
- o Appreciating the power of visualisation and manifesting

It all works.

And then there is ego! … Having the attitude of "If I'm good then people will find me", I agree, is positive mindset, however it comes across as expectation rather than coming from a place of serving your clients.

- o A positive mindset
- o Visualisation
- o Manifesting
- o Believing in your expertise
- o Being aware of the value you bring to your clients
- o Taking massive aligned action

All of these are essential to achieving any goal in life, or in your business.

And now it comes to the investment your client will make into your programme itself. WOW, this is such a big topic! I am not going to say you should charge £88 or £8,888! What I am going to say is tackle your mindset. I have, very briefly, shared how to use the Energy Alignment Method in a previous Chapter. EAM will help you counteract those negative vibrations to come from a place of positivity when sharing your message, marketing posts, talking about your programme and closing the sale. I'll say again what I said a few moments ago ….

Believe in yourself!
Believe in your programme.
Believe in your ability to make the difference for our client.

Allow your clients the honour of making the decision themselves if to pay your investment or not. They will balance their investment with the promised outcome of your programme, hence why it is important to be truthful in your marketing material and not over promise.

If you are not attracting paying clients, it is unlikely to be the fee that is the problem. Put the spotlight on your marketing message, or where you are targeting your marketing.

People will pay for what THEY want, it is up to us to market our value and share the outcome they will achieve by completing our programme. Changing your mindset to realising every opportunity is a marketing opportunity, understanding your value and why people buy from you is a real game changer.

Return to your Ideal Client Avatar work, at the beginning of the book and have a look at what you wrote down to the following questions ....
- o Do you understand what the challenges are you help people overcome, the problems you solve?
- o Do you understand what you do to help people, the value you bring?
- o Do you understand what's in it for the client, what the benefits are for them, the results you deliver?

If you look at these answers then you have a lot of information for your marketing. Use the answers in your sales copy, sales conversations, your elevator pitch, your free offer, on your website, in your articles and blogs.

Every opportunity is a marketing opportunity!

Success is all in the marketing:
- o Resist talking about degrees and certificates – talk about the RESULTS you deliver.
- o Complete your marketing sentence "And this is so great because ......" then you are thinking like a marketeer.
- o It is essential to be able to talk about the VALUE and RESULTS you achieve through clients following your programme, otherwise your fees will probably remain small.

It's the value and results that attract the investment from clients. I can't emphasise that enough!

Remember, by marketing you ARE serving your clients. Why? They may not realise there is a solution to their current situation. They may need you to show them the way and what life is like when they resolve the problem they are experiencing.

It is essential that your marketing material is not written whilst you are in a place of lack or in a place of need. Otherwise, your message will come across as pushy. You can overcome this by using the Energy Alignment Method I spoke of in an earlier Chapter. If you are stuck then you can book a session with me through my website www.stephaniethompsoncoaching.com

Referring back to the previous Chapter where I introduced the Energy Alignment Method technique and on the assumption that your sway is true (forwards for yes and backwards for no) here is a question to ask your energy before writing your marketing copy. Do follow the whole technique described earlier though.

Ask "Do I have any resistance to writing my marketing copy?".

If you swayed forward for yes then repeat this statement 3 times:

"I am ready to release, any and all resistance to writing my marketing copy. I release it from my energy in all forms, on all levels, at all points in time".

Check the resistance has been release by asking the original question. "Do I have any resistance to writing my marketing copy?". Fingers crossed you now sway backwards for no.

Here is a brief statement to repeat 3 times to bring in the positive energy

"I am ready to be fully aligned with my message, for my marketing copy to flow easily and connect deeply with my Ideal Client".

You can also use EAM to release any resistance to charging your chosen fee too.

If you have any questions, please contact me at stephanie@stephaniethompsoncoaching.com or you can find out more about booking EAM sessions with me through my website www.stephaniethompsoncoaching.com

And here is one final thing I want to share with you before closing this Chapter …

I know when I very first started my coaching business, I got myself sooooo hooked up on Terms and Conditions, Refund Policies, GDPR, Cookies Policy, all sorts of things! Yes, I agree some are necessary, some are non-essential too, but the biggest tip I can give you is "Keep things as simple as possible".

By using an online marketing business system, they tend to include a GDPR statement for you.

A Refund Policy can be very straightforward such as:
This is an electronic online programme where you gain instant access, we do not offer a refund policy, however you can cancel your subscription at any time.

Terms and Conditions may need to be a little more detailed but try to limit it to one page, by keeping it very simple and straightforward. Here are some items you may wish to consider including ......

- o Clients need to do their part by taking aligned action each step of the way.
- o Cancellation policy – can cancel a meeting up to 24-hours prior. If cancelled within the 24 hours, or are a no-show the call will be considered complete.
- o Rules of the call. The call is 30 minutes so to make sure you get everything ready for the call, ring the coach promptly (if you are late making contact the call will still finish at the allotted time and not run over) come prepared with the progress made against last week's actions, any questions and your plan for this week. Please phone from an environment where you can speak freely.
- o How to contact you outside of the allocated diary times. For example, via email with the relevant address or a phone number with an associated voice mail. Be clear how long before you provide an answer. For example, "Responses are normally made within 48 hours".
- o The aim of the call. If there is any pre-work required make sure the client receives all the relevant information, or working links to access the detail.

And finally. something to bring a smile …

Don't Quit by Edgar Albert Guest

When things go wrong, as they sometimes will
When the road you're trudging seems all uphill
When funds are low and debts are high
And you want to smile but have to sigh
When care is pressing you down a bit

100

Rest if you must but don't you quit!

Life is queer with its twists and turns,
As every one of us sometimes learns.
And many a failure turns about,
When she might have won had she stuck it out.
Don't give up, though the pace seems slow,
You may succeed with another blow!

Success is failure turned inside out,
The silver tint of the clouds of doubt.
And you never can tell how close you are,
It may be near when it seems so far.
So, stick to the fight when you're hardest hit,
It's when things seem worst that **YOU MUST NOT QUIT!**

As we draw to the end of stage seven, hopefully, you have gained some insight on:

o   Investment made by the client into your programmes. The answer is .... It doesn't matter how much, it's all about delivering real value. Believing in yourself! Believe in your programmes! Believe in your ability to make the difference for your clients!

o   Share about the OUTCOME of working with you, the benefits, the What's In It For Me factor.

o   Understand your Ideal Client's hell and heaven, then take them on a journey through your marketing material because they may just not realise that life could be different, they may not even realise there is a solution for them! It is up to you to show them the way.

I would love to hear about your success, so please do drop me a note to stephanie@stephaniethompsoncoaching.com

Also, if you have any questions, please send them to the same email address above

By taking action
we learn quicker,
move further faster
and make a
difference sooner.

Chapter 9 –

Are you reluctant to get visible?

I just have to start this Chapter with a true story. You would NOT believe how I started to get visible!!!!

It came to doing my very first Facebook Live and I just could not face it. I bottled out and decided to record and upload to Facebook instead. I knew what I wanted to say but all I could see was myself on the screen! Twenty-three takes later and it was not going well!

In my wisdom, I decided to print out a photograph, on to a large letter sized piece of paper, of one of my best friends. Then where one of her eyes were, I cut out a small circle. With the help of some BluTac I positioned the hole over the camera on my computer and I was set to go.

I could not see myself on screen and I was talking to a very friendly face, who is very supportive of my work. It still took me several more takes! But I eventually finished my task and uploaded the video.

Unfortunately, the story does not end there. That evening my exact same friend was coming for tea. She arrived and as I was cooking dinner and we were chatting, she spotted the photograph of her – with her eye cut out!!! Then I had to explain exactly what I had done and why. Fortunately, she found it absolutely hilarious and was so delighted she was able to help, even though she hadn't actually done anything.

I continued using her photograph for a little while, but eventually I built my confidence and now-a-days I jump onto zoom or Facebook Live without a worry! So, if you are reluctant to get visible, I know EXACTLY what you are going through.

It all starts with self-sabotage, doesn't it? And you come up with every excuse imaginable.
I'm having a bad hair day
I've got no makeup on
I can't hold my phone still

What are your supposed to talk about?
I look fat on screen
The sound is wrong
I haven't got anything to wear
The background is wrong
I can't do this
I don't know what to say
What if I stutter?
What if I forget what I am saying?
How long are you supposed to talk for?
The children won't keep quiet long enough
What if the doorbell rings for that delivery I am expecting?

And the list goes on and on, excuse after excuse after excuse. Oh yes, I have heard a hundred different excuses and most of them came out of my own mouth!!!!!

To be honest, they really do feel like valid excuses at the time so, let's see what we can do about tackling this situation shall we?

There are 3 different things to address ......
- o Mindset
- o Appearance
- o Content

Let's work on MINDSET first and I will say, before we get started, it is not necessary to use all of the follow suggestions. Pick one, or two, that resonate with you. Experiment and see what works best for you.

There are so many different techniques you can use to adjust your mindset. I found meditation helped me a huge amount when I first started out. The meditation helped to ground me and keep me centred It helped to conquer my nerves and quieten my mind. I found spending time reflecting very peaceful and calming. Everything slows down, there is no rush and I feel more able.

Meditation can take many forms. You can have a led meditation, or total silence, or accompanying music. Whatever suits you best I would definitely recommend it. Not sure where to start? My go-to is Dauchsy meditations on YouTube, however there are dozens of different ones to choose from. You need to find something that resonates with you and achieves that calming of nerves.

I then follow the meditation with a visualisation exercise. Again, this can be a led visualisation, or one you do yourself. You can always record your own led visualisation too, there are some amazing Apps available now-a-days.

I would like to share, at this point, once you get into the swing of being visible then these preparations will become defunct. However, when you are starting out there really is a need. I know because I was soooooo reluctant to get on camera myself at first!

Here is a brief visualisation right now, only if you are in a safe place to do so, certainly not whilst you are driving or operating machines of any kind ....

Sit back in your chair, feet flat on the floor, take a few deep breaths
Close your eyes and feel your body relaxing back into the chair
And I want you to start playing a movie in your head
Just take a moment to look at your surroundings
You are in a comfortable chair
You can see the laptop or phone in front of you
You have your notes pinned to one side
You have everything set up and ready to press record
You scan your body to see if there is anything tense, if you have any nerves. And if you do, you just smooth them away, by taking a few deep breaths
You check in and realise just how confident you feel
You have done your preparations; you know what you are going to say and you're ready
Still playing that movie in your head
You feel yourself taking a breath
You press the record button
And you begin speaking
You speak with confidence
You smile at the camera
You share your message, as if you are talking to a friend sitting in the room with you.
There isn't any paraphernalia around, you are just sharing with your friend sat there in the same room with you
You chat away, easily and without hesitation, taking your viewers on a journey through your message
And before you even realise it you are coming to an end
Now you are saying goodbye to your clients and sharing with them the call-to-action to get in touch with you for more information

The conversation flows smoothly and easily
You come from a place of giving and sharing
The whole call has been flawless
And now the call has finished
You lean forward to stop the recording
You relax back in your chair and take a drink whilst the recording is
processing
And you click the share button.
There is no need to watch it through
You know the recording has gone well
That all your preparation has created a faultless recording and you are
happy to share with your audience straight away
All has gone well.

Take a few deep breaths and slowly open your eyes. Come back into the room.

How do you feel now? Any nerves? Any worries about going on camera?

Visualisation is a VERY powerful tool. Paul McKenna quotes in his book "Change your life in 7 days" ... *"For centuries people thought it was impossible to run a four-minute mile. Then on 6 May 1954 Roger Bannister did what all great pioneers do - he made the impossible happen. Within a year of Bannister breaking the four-minute mile, 37 other people around the world had done so as well. In the following year, an incredible 300 runners broke through that previously impenetrable barrier. The finest minds of the age had believed it was impossible to do and their beliefs became a self-fulfilling prophecy. It took one counter-example - one person proving that what they had previously thought could not be done was possible - for everyone else to tap into that possibility within themselves. Bannister was no different to any other runner except for one thing ..... He visualised achieving the goal and he believed he was able to do it."*

I have to admit I have used visualisation many times, particularly when I was getting up on stages around the world sharing my knowledge with huge audiences. I continue to use visualisation too. It is one of the things that helps me create such a compelling vision for my life and my business. I love it and I hope it helps you too.

Maybe you are not one for using meditation or visualisation, in which case writing might be for you. This could be in the form of journaling or writing a letter.

I know when my marriage broke down writing letters really helped me ease the emotions within. Don't worry I didn't post the letters. In fact, I think I even burnt them virtually straight away because I did not want the negative energy around me. I wrote to express my inner turmoil and "get it off my chest". Sometimes it would go on for pages and pages but, when I had finished, I felt emotionally purged and so much better; more able to cope.

I digress yet again. Sorry. Let's get back to the written word, in whatever format, to help you clear those worries from your mind, ready to "get on camera".

Sometimes it is good to have a few statements to write against, to help start the process, so here are some suggested questions for you to journal on ....
- o *What do I want to say in my recording?*
- o *How do I feel about doing the recording?*
- o *How can I boost my confidence before recording?*
- o *What can I do to make it easier to record?*
- o *What are the positives for doing this recording?*
- o *What could go wrong and how would I deal with it?*
- o *Who can I talk with, or, where can I find information, to help me overcome my nerves and get started?*
- o *How will I feel once I have shared the recording?*
- o *What impact will my recording have with my Ideal Client?*
- o *What will I talk about next time I do a recording?*

The best piece of advice I can give you is:

**Life isn't about waiting for the storm to pass.
It's about learning to dance in the rain.**

There are other techniques that can help too, such as Breathing or Tapping. In fact, I have just put a search into Google for calming nerves before a presentation and there are just under half a million options, so there is no excuse to procrastinate any longer. Now is the time to take action!

Self-sabotage can keep you invisible too. You know, those mind monkeys, the negative inner critic. I am sure you know by now I am a great advocate of the Energy Alignment Method. Using EAM will help to release limiting thoughts and beliefs, the fear of being visible, the fear of being judged, the fear of being criticised, the fear of not being good enough, the fear of being seen as an imposter and the list goes on. EAM can help with all of these so please hop on my website to find out more at www.stephaniethompsoncoaching.com

Hopefully I have given you sufficient ideas to help with turning your mindset around when it comes to going visible.

When I first started going live on Facebook I had so much noise in my head from my inner critic that I needed to squash it!!! First thing I did was tackle the negativity using the mindset techniques I have just been talking about.

Next was to focus on APPEARANCE and get into some practicalities.

If you can see it on the screen then so can your audience! The background does not miraculously disappear when others view, so here are some things to think about ......

Set the camera up where you are going to record then step behind the camera and see what it sees. Use a critical eye, really see what you are looking at.

Is the background appropriate for your business? For example:
- Is the background that looks out over your garden a builder's yard? Especially if you are a landscape gardener!
- Do the cupboard doors have paint peeling off them? Especially when you are a painter and decorator?
- Is there a pile of ironing waiting to be done?
- A half-made cup of tea, mouldy oranges, or a bag of shopping in view?
- Are there any titles on the bookshelf you would prefer others didn't see?

There are several options to address these problems such as:
- Tidy everywhere up and keep it tidy, so it doesn't become a huge task to go live
- Create a backdrop you can use, which could be a curtain that you draw, or a screen you put up, or have a background of your logo printed
- Zoom has the ability to change your background, however it may not always give the professional image you wish for your business

Now sit in front of the camera and really inspect the background around your body

- o Do you have a plant growing out of your head?
- o Does it look like you are just about to be stabbed by knives sitting on your kitchen wall (we don't really want you looking like you have the sword of Damocles hanging over you, do we?!!)
- o Do you have a mirror behind you that is showing you are sitting in your pyjama bottoms, or reflecting a messy room to the audience?

I have had a situation where someone was laying, front down on their bed talking with me, which was fine, they looked perfectly presentable – except they were naked and I could see their bare bottom in the full-length wardrobe mirror behind them. It was a tad disconcerting I can tell you!!!!!

Be aware of the lighting.

If you have your camera pointing towards the window then your face will probably be in darkness, because of the back-light. Either move your camera to a different place, or ensure you have really good lighting in front of you. It is preferable to have natural daylight, but it is not always practical, so switch on every light you can, even bring lamps in from other rooms. It is not always necessary to invest in expensive lighting kits.

If your image appears dark in the small picture of you on the screen, then the viewer can see even less.

The angle of the camera is also something to think about. There is nothing worse than someone talking to you and all you can do is stare up their nose! Ideally the camera should be at eye level or slightly higher. Place your camera on a stack of books if necessary. It is well worth having the camera slightly higher, so you are lifting your chin slightly, which reduces a double chin if you are unfortunate to have one.

Do try and reduce as much camera shake as possible. It can make some viewers feel quite seasick. If you have a tripod, use it, although it is not always practical, so the other option is to lean your arm onto something like a wall, or a gate if you are outside, to keep the tremble to a minimum .

If you do a lot of action shots, or talks whilst you are out walking, then investment in a Camera Gimbal Stabilizer might be necessary.

Reduce as many interruptions or distractions as you can such as:

- Turning off notifications on your phone, tablet and laptop.
- Putting a sign on the door telling the family not to interrupt because you are filming.
- Making sure the dishwasher and washing machine are not running, or the grass is being cut outside the window.

And finally, "to wear, or not to wear" make-up. This is purely down to personal choice. If you don't normally wear make-up and it would be a huge performance to put make-up on then don't bother. It depends on the image you want to portray. What I will say is wearing foundation, eyebrow pencil and lipstick does make a huge difference to what is seen on screen.

Being confident in your surroundings and how you look and feel contributes hugely to your confidence on camera. Take the time to understand what you feel most comfortable with and fits in with your lifestyle. Please know that we all make mistakes, we do things in a rush, we don't always see what is behind us. However, by taking time to plan it out at the beginning, so you know what to be aware of, will help. All these hints and tips that I am sharing with you, you do not have to do every single time, because eventually it will become second nature. But whilst you are building up to doing lives, hopefully they will help you conquer those nerves a little.

And the final topic is CONTENT.

You know your own content and what you are sharing with your clients and potential clients, however I would like to chat a little about the structure of your content.

First things first is to know who you are talking with – your Ideal Client, which has been covered in a previous Chapter. Focus on talking to your "one client" from the Four Ones referred to earlier in the book. Share information they want to know and also share how you can help them.

Before you record plan what you want to have achieved at the end of the recording?

Think about how you are going to capture their attention so they stay and watch all of your live/recording?

What is the story you are going to share, that will help them understand what you are trying to explain to them?

I am sure you will have picked up that I try and intersperse my sharing of information with some stories. Well, what are the stories you are going to use? Or it might be facts and data, rather than stories, that is more appropriate to your message.

And the last piece is the "call-to-action". Remember my Four Ones? One Client. One Platform. One Message. One Call-to-action. So, what is the call-to-action you are going to ask the clients to take?

The Facebook algorithm, I believe at the point of writing this book, prefers Live's to be at least three minutes long; no longer than six. If you are trying to capture potential client's attention then aim for three minutes.

One final thing to share before we end this Chapter … The two enemies of Procrastination and Perfectionism. Both will stop your making progress. They will hold you back, keep you small, and stop you being successful.

I shared my Procrastination shame in a previous Chapter. Here is a story about my hiccup with perfectionism ….

It took a Director, of a multi-million pound global company, to explain to me that trying to get something perfect was impossible. The conversation went something like this …
"Stephanie, do you have that report yet?"
"It's not quite ready".
"You've been saying that all week. Are you trying to make it perfect?"
"Well, I just want to check it one more time".
"Stephanie! Nothing is ever perfect. You are spending all this time and the minute someone else reads it they will spot something, or won't like the way you have laid it out, or the font you have used. It could be any excuse. The thing is, because you have done so much work on it, you will then take the criticism personally. So, to avoid all that hurt and to keep the wheels turning, as long as the facts are correct get it distributed so decisions can be made".

Might this story resonate with you?

So, it is better to take imperfect action and make progress rather than striving for perfection, which, by the way, is another form of procrastination!

I can assure you, you learn a lot faster by getting something "out there"! We all have to start at some point, we cannot keep putting off the inevitable. In the words of the amazing Joseph McClendon III "Fortune favours the bold". Or, to be more blunt, "money loves speed"!

As we draw to the end of stage eight, hopefully, you have gained some insight on:

- o Mindset – change your overwhelmed mindset by using meditation, visualisation, journaling, EAM or other techniques that may help. I am a big advocate of visualisation and recall that story I told you about Roger Bannister running the first 4-minute mile achieved through visualising.
- o Appearance – check your background and the angle of your camera
- o Content – be prepared and take your viewers on a journey remembering to include a call-to-action at the end, if appropriate.
- o My procrastination shame, how I was cured of perfectionism and how I first started doing lives by talking to a photo of my best friend.

I have shared all these hints and tips but at the end of the day being visible is not about being perfect. It's about being real and letting people see the authentic you.

When you very first start out, work in a medium that you are most comfortable with and build up to being visible on camera, which is the quickest way to build "know, like and trust" with your potential community.

I would love to hear about your success, so please do drop me a note to stephanie@stephaniethompsoncoaching.com

Also, if you have any questions, please send them to the same email address above.

Chapter 10 –

How to find your tribe

Building your tribe can feel a bit of a daunting task. Where on earth do you start to find where your Ideal Client hangs out? Keep reading to find out more.

Hop onto your Facebook Group page and click Group Insights, where you can glean all sorts of information such as:
   o   Which day(s) your community are most engaged.
   o   Which time(s) of those days you get most interactions.

Admittedly this can be influenced by when you post. However, at the beginning of your journey, you can probably see a possible pattern to give your posts a better chance of being seen by your Ideal Clients.

A Facebook Group also enables you to schedule posts. This means you can co-ordinate and schedule your posts with when your Ideal Clients are most active, to increase your engagement.

Then there are Facebook Pages, where you can also click "Insights" which, again, shares multiple pieces of information. The main ones I use include the age and gender of people engaging with my posts.

I was at a conference recently and a gentleman stood up to share his experience about understanding his Facebook Statistics. When starting out, helping people prepare for their driving theory test, he thought his Ideal Client would be gents aged 16 to 21 and he built his business marketing copy based on this. Once he had been running his business a little while he reviewed his statistics again and had quite a revelation. He found, according to the Insights, the people viewing and interacting with his posts were actually females aged 20 to 30. Taking this on board he tweaked his marketing copy accordingly and his business rocketed.

Like Facebook Groups, you can also schedule posts on Facebook Pages to improve your chances of engagement.

Viewing these statistics can be very informative and you can use the data to measure your growth, engagement and reach, amongst other things.

My recommendation is understand where are you starting from? It is always good to take a note of your current numbers, that way you can see how far you have progressed. We spend so much time looking forwards that we forget how far we have come. It is crucial to get those celebratory dopamine hits to maintain your drive and momentum.

Don't overwhelm yourself with huge amounts of data though. Keep it simple, use basic information such as:
- o How many contacts
- o What age range
- o Which days
- o What times
- o Gender

Please don't over complicate things by spreading yourself too thinly, across multiple social media channels, you will wear yourself out. Referring back to my Four Ones - pick one social media channel. get it established, even automated, then move onto the next one. On the new platform use the information you already know is successful and build.

How to communicate with your Ideal Client Avatar is also an important factor contributing to building your tribe.

There are 3 main ways to engage with your client. I would recommend you pick the one you are most comfortable with and then build in the other formats, as you gain more confidence.

The options are:
- o Written posts – Blogs. Articles. Workbooks.
- o Audio posts – Podcasts.
- o Visual posts - Facebook lives. Video. In person.

In a nutshell, share what you can help with and why, plus where they can find you. Talk as if you are talking with a friend. Save the "how" for your programme; it is the "how" your Ideal Client will pay for.

The reason for communicating with your Ideal Client is to build a relationship with them. Let them get to "know, like and trust" you.

Remember,
if they know and like you, they will listen,
it is only once they trust you, will they buy.

Starting with your preferred media hopefully means fewer nerves, so you can concentrate on building the relationship.

Hint - The quickest way to build a relationship is by video because they can see you, hear you and get a feel for your personality.

I saw a quote from Andy Harrington recently. Andy trains in public speaking and crafting your story. The quote said: *"If you want to make it big and turn passion into profit, you'll need to create a business that begins by offering an information product that is written, audio and visual format".*

I think his comment sums it up perfectly. By sharing your message in all 3 mediums you are also hitting all the different learning styles of your Ideal Client.

Another way of engaging with you Ideal Client is through networking. Typically, people buy from people they know, which is why it is essential to build that "know, like and trust". The connections can come from social media, or in-person events.

How do you find local networking groups? Tap into your browser "networking groups near me" and various options will appear. You will find profession-specific networks, small business networks, business-to-business networks; breakfast networks, activity networks, and the list goes on.

They all have one thing in common - to introduce you to other people and allow the opportunity to share your business offering.

Networking will certainly encourage you to refine your "60-second elevator pitch", sometimes known as your "value proposition". You know, the one where you are riding up in an elevator with your most Ideal Client and you have 60-seconds to sell yourself and your business before they step off the elevator. Your pitch needs to be succinct, pique their interest and provide them with enough information that they want to know more.

If you are going to attend live networking events, I would suggest you should invest in some business cards, which are not necessary for on-line events.

Yes, there are usually fees involved in attending networking events. It can even run into the hundreds and thousands of pounds per year. Fortunately, you can often attend as a guest once or twice for a small sum to cover drinks, and food if provided. Doing this provides you the opportunity to see how you feel at the event, if your Ideal Client is there, if you like the format before you invest.

Networking on-line is also a fantastic opportunity to share your message to a wider audience reaching into Australia, USA, across Europe and the UK, plus every other country in between.

You can find specific groups, where your Ideal Clients might hang out, by searching on Facebook using some key words you have identified through the Ideal Client hell and heaven questions you answered earlier. Do ensure, with Facebook Groups you want to engage with to set notifications to "see first".

Do not overwhelm yourself by seeking to join dozens and dozens of groups. Be selective. Choose groups that seem to be active (posts per day) and has a decent number of followers. Seven is probably too small, whereas 8000 is possibly too large, depending on the topic. Use your judgement on what suits you and your business.

Begin by responding to posts, in your chosen groups, regularly and consistently. Share advice, offer opinions, suggest options, however do not pitch your products or services just yet, unless that is what is being asked for. You do not need to generate posts in the group yet either.

The aim is to build a relationship with the community, you want them to get to "know, like and trust" you.

A tip - also pick a couple of groups that have regular posts that ask you to share your links, freebies and offers. Within my own Facebook Group, at various points throughout the week or month I put up posts so you can share your freebies and pitch your offerings. If you are not in my free group then join quick, it would be wonderful to welcome you https://www.facebook.com/groups/StephanieThompsonGetFocusedFastAttractingClients

In this day and age of technology, 8-second attention spans and multiple channels, if you do not market then your Ideal Client cannot find you, so be consistently visible.

It is very easy to become a stalker on social media. You stay quiet and see what everyone else is doing or saying; then the magical post comes where you can "share your freebie". You take a big breath and you share your link. Then you wait with bated breath for that first download. But nothing comes. You face your inner demons of not being good enough, nobody wants what I have to offer and you go back to stalking, or worse still you throw it all up and stick with the very stressful 9-5 job!

I can assure you "you ARE good enough"!

I can assure you "they DO want what you offer"!

The difference is they do not know who you are. That "know, like and trust" has not been built and so they just scroll past. They do not stop to see what you are sharing.

Sorry, but there is no magical formula - it is purely and simply "be visible consistently". Share what you are doing, share your knowledge, build that "know, like and trust". Also, the relationship doesn't happen overnight. It builds over time. This is why being consistent is essential.

With this in mind, what is your marketing strategy to increase your visibility? Some gurus will say post four times a day! To be honest, that would wear me out, because I am an introvert. I like people don't get me wrong, but I do love my own company; the quiet, the solitude. So, for me to have to think of something to say four times a day would be my worst nightmare. Thank goodness for scheduling is all I can say. Over the years I have built up a wonderful social media library and now to post three or four times a day is not a big task. For the more extrovert amongst us, then posting on a daily basis might be absolutely perfect.

What I am saying here is play to your strengths. If you want to be present for your tribe one day per week, for 90-minutes, on video, then do that, but do it consistently week after week because it takes time to gain momentum. If you want to post about Angel cards every day then do so, but don't stop after two weeks - be constant so your Ideal Client learns to trust that you will always be there for them. Be consistent.

So, what is your marketing strategy to increase your visibility? To post daily? Weekly? Thrice daily? Plan the time, in your diary, to do your social media so you remain consistent.

Should your posts be public or just to those who friend you? On your personal profile, I totally understand why you would want to keep your posts private so only your friends see them, especially if they are personal posts.

Facebook Business Pages are usually public, however people are reluctant to bare their souls in public, so you may not get the deeper engagement you are hoping for.

Facebook Groups can be set to public or private. It is the private groups where lots of engagement takes place. The Facebook Group is where you nurture your future paying clients. But how do you get your Ideal Client to know about the Group? By sharing the link wherever you can. Ah yes Stephanie, but what about the Facebook Algorithm? One of the brilliant things is that your Group is still within Facebook and therefore the Facebook Algorithm will not penalise you for using that link in your posts.

You can post on your personal profile what is happening in your group. Make it exciting and share what they are missing out on. Make them curious. At the end of your post mention that they are welcome to join and provide a link to your Facebook Group. Make it as easy as possible for potential clients to come and find out more.

You can also post the link to your Facebook Group into your public Facebook Business Page. To attract potential clients into your Facebook Group you would include the Group link in your posts in your profile page, business page and other's groups.

Within the Facebook Group, and on the Facebook Page, there is a facility to invite your friends to join too.

Remember –
a client is more likely to take action
after they have seen your message
roughly SEVENTEEN times!!!!

In this day and age of social media and 8-second attention spans, you need to be consistent for potential clients to notice you. So, as well as posts, blogs, vlogs, newsletters, graphics, Facebook Lives, here are some other opportunities that may come your way to appear in front of your Ideal Client.

Be a guest speaker or guest expert in another person's Facebook Group or Page.

Often, in other people's groups, you will see an appeal for Guest Experts or Speakers. This is usually your opportunity to talk, for up to an hour, on your expert area. I have appeared as a Guest Expert in Australia, USA and UK Facebook groups. I saw the request, responded saying I would be willing to support and then followed their process through; some hosts are very relaxed, others are quite organised to minute detail. I followed through their instructions and was able to share my message in their groups. The Australia appearance ultimately resulted in my becoming an international, number one, best-selling co-author, as well as attracting many Australian participants into my group and onto my 5-day challenge. The USA appearance did not result in such an accolade as a best-selling book; however, I did attract more into my group and ultimately onto my programmes.

Remember Facebook prioritises Lives, so being a guest expert in another group is a great way to increase your reach.

Podcasts (audio) and Interviews (live) are another opportunity. Much like being a guest speaker or guest expert, you will see appeals from Facebook Group hosts wanting speakers.

Often with a podcast and interview the host provides you with a list of questions prior so you can prepare your answers and, with the hosts encouragement, you can share the work you do and the benefits your clients achieve during your answers. I have been fortunate enough to be invited to do both podcasts and interviews in the UK, Germany and USA, resulting in my Facebook Group community growing. In the name of reciprocity, it is polite to invite the host to do similar in your Facebook Group, if you can furnish that opportunity.

Expanding your reach, organically, is a great way to start getting visible. Organically means you are not paying for advertising. Encouraging engagement of your community is essential, which can be achieved in multiple ways.
o   Ask the community to "love" posts rather than "like" posts.

- Always, always, always respond to anyone who takes the trouble to comment on your post, but don't let it overtake your life to the exclusion of building your business.
- If at all possible, respond with a question so the person comes back with an answer. This increases engagement and building that know like and trust.

Wherever possible engage via Facebook live or video. Ideally upload the video directly into Facebook, rather than sharing from an outside site like YouTube, Vimeo or Wistia etc. Sharing links from those platforms means you are taking the viewer away from Facebook and therefore you will slip down the algorithm scale. Keeping people engaged within Facebook is key.

At the time of writing, Facebook Lives achieve 6 times, yes 6 times, more engagement than a recorded video. Videos are viewed more than text posts. So, if you are wanting to expand your reach then make sure you use Facebook Live, or if you haven't quite got your confidence yet then an uploaded video is the next best thing.

There are posts in my Facebook Group where you are encouraged to come and develop your skills to do a Facebook Live, so take advantage and let's start seeing more of you in my group – https://www.facebook.com/groups/StephanieThompsonGetFocusedFastAttractingClients

Be aware if you do a Facebook Live in a private Facebook group the live is only accessible within the group. However, if you do a Live on your Facebook Page you can then share it to other profiles, groups and pages.

As we draw to the end of stage nine, hopefully, you have gained some insight on:
- How to find your tribe
- Facebook Insights to reveal information about your client's behaviour on Facebook
- Basic statistics
- Three ways to engage – written, audio and video
- Networking – locally and on-line.
- Sharing posts
- Being a guest speaker or guest expert.

I would love to hear about your success, so please do drop me a note to stephanie@stephaniethompsoncoaching.com

Also, if you have any questions, please send them to the same email address above.

REPEAT AFTER ME ....

Today I am going to be FABULOUS
Tomorrow I'll be SENSATIONAL
Wednesday I'll be WONDERFUL
Thursday I am going to be INCREDIBLE
Friday I am going to be MAGNIFICENT
Saturday I'll be COURAGEOUS
Sunday I am going to be INTREPID

Chapter 11 –

How does social media support your message?

Let's begin with your social media profile and how it supports you. Your Social Media profile is your business card to the world. It is your shop window for all to view. What does it say about you?

With technology as it is today, there is so much that can be found out about you from your profiles and public posts, before your Ideal Client joins you. Pay particular attention to your profile on the platforms you are using to connect with your Ideal Clients.

The things to look out for are:
o The setting – is it private or public; being public makes you much more visible of course.
o Does your profile make it really clear what you do? For example, in the past I have been a buyer, but now I am a coach so I needed to update my profiles accordingly.
o Does your profile share links to your relevant social media pages, website and blog site? Please be aware you can build your business very easily without a website, don't worry.

Make it as easy as possible for your potential clients to find you and identify with you.

The next step is to build connection with your Ideal Client and ultimately for them to purchase from you. This is achieved through building "know, like and trust", which I have shared in previous Chapters.

What is your connection strategy in other groups where your Ideal Clients hang out?
o Are you going to interact with their posts?
o Are you going to post questions?
o Are you going to share information?
o Are you going to engage in the group daily/weekly/monthly?

There is no right or wrong answer other than you must be consistent. When deciding on the level of consistency, take into account if you are able to maintain that commitment long-term.

A strategy is also required for your own social media pages and groups. Again, whatever you decide is right, as long as you are consistent.
o   Are you going to post questions and seek their input? How often?
o   Are you going to post polls so you can gain information? How often?
o   Are you going to share a video every day/week/month? What are the topics?
o   Are you going to put a call-to-action on every single post?
o   Are you going to be your authentic self and share personal information about your life/family/friends/activities/etc.?

These are some of the questions to think about for your own social media content strategy.

Also, think about how you are going to connect with your clients? I have shared previously, the options are audio, visual, written, graphics and also the platform you use may also have a preference, for example Instagram and Pinterest work with graphics very nicely.

Wherever it is appropriate add a call-to-action, even something as simple as "put an emoji in the comments". A call-to-action builds engagement with your client relationship. Those that have taken the action have an interest in what you are talking about, so it helps you understand if you are on the right track. Without wanting to add to the pressure of becoming visible, it is the posts that create intrigue and captures the imagination that gains the interest.

Are you engaging with your client's imagination? Are you attracting their 8-second attention span enough to make them stop, look AND want to know more?

Keep an eye on your Facebook Page Insight statistics. Work out which posts are gaining the most engagement and do more of the same. Remember every audience is different and what works for one coach may not work for another. Experiment until you find a message that works and resonates with your Ideal Client.

Creating Social Media content can seem an enormous task, however it is quite straightforward once you know how. Grab hold of a pile of post-its, a pen and clear a space on the table in front of you. I am going to share with you a simple formula on how to create social media content.

At the top of the post-it write ASK – then write a question that will engage with your audience and help you get to know your Ideal Clients better. Questions might include:
- o Who is your Ideal Client?
- o What 3 things are essential when setting up as a coach?
- o How do you overcome procrastination?
- o When are you are your most creative?

Write 4 post-its with a question on each. Place them in a column on the table in front of you.

At the top of the next post-it write GIVE – then write what piece of information you will give to your audience and help your Ideal Client get to know and like you.
- o These are hints and tips that you can GIVE. Maybe snippets from the freebie you offer.

Write 4 post-its and place them in a column on the table, next to the ASK post-its.

At the top of the post-it write FUN – then write a random fun question to gain engagement with your audience. Questions might include:
- o What is your favourite book and why?
- o Where do you love to go on holiday?
- o Are you a procrastinator or a perfectionist?
- o How do you spend your down time?

Write 4 post-its, with a fun question on each, and place them in a column, next to the GIVE post-its.

At the top of the post-it write MY STORY – then think about things you are willing to share with your audience. This is often part of your journey from your hell to your heaven. Things you might include here are:
- o Your aha moments.
- o How you felt before you made the transformation.
- o How you feel now you have made the transformation.
- o The emotions you experienced making the changes you needed to make.

Write 4 post-its and place them in a column, next to the FUN post-its.

At the top of the post-it write MY IDEAL CLIENT – then share who you work with, why you work with them. Things you might include are:

- New female coaches aged 45 plus … because there is a life after the nest empties!
- Coaches starting their first business … because there is so much information available and I just wanted someone to show me step-by-step what to do.
- Women who have more to give to the world, who want to share their knowledge and experience. Women who felt they had lost themselves … Because we are beautiful souls and have so much to offer to those following in our steps.

Write 4 post-its and place them in a column, next to the MY STORY post-its.

At the top of the post-it write TESTIMONIALS – then share what others have said about working with you. Things you might include are:
- Social proof photo of a testimonial.
- Excerpt from an email a happy client sent to you, with their permission of course.
- A video from a happy client singing your praises.

Write 4 post-its and place them in a column, next to the MY IDEAL CLIENT post-its.

At the top of the post-it write OFFER – then share what you are offering to your Ideal Client.
Things you might include are:
- A link to your freebie.
- A link to your calendar for your Ideal Client to book a discovery call.
- A post about your upcoming event and how they can register their interest.
- A post about your early-bird offer and how they can sign up.

Write 4 post-its and place them in a column, next to the TESTIMONIAL post-its.

At the top of the post-it write VIDEO – then jot down topics you could talk about. Things you might include are:
- My procrastination shame.
- Why 80% is good enough.
- The importance of 168.
- Henry Ford's study.

Write 4 post-its and place them in a column, next to the MY OFFER post-its.

At the top of the post-it write BLOG – then jot down which blog snippets you are going to share. Things you might include are:

- Chasing Shiny Penny dreams.
- Make the space and see what happens.
- Is your big why compelling enough?
- Do I need a freebie giveaway?

These are all headings from my website if you would like to know what I wrote hop onto

www.stephaniethompsoncoaching.com

Write 4 post-its and place them in a column, next to the VIDEO post-its.

At the top of the post-it write MONDAY – Headings you might include are:
- Manifesting Monday.
- Blitz it Monday.
- Getting it done Monday.
- Intention setting Monday.

Write 4 post-its with these heading, a bullet point on what you will talk about that day and place them in a column, next to the BLOG post-its.

At the top of the post-it write TUESDAY – Headings you might include are:
- Tuesday Tip.
- Useful things to know Tuesday.
- Top Tip Tuesday.
- Things to know Tuesday.

Write 4 post-its with these headings with a bullet point on what you will talk about that day and place them in a column, next to the MONDAY post-its.

At the top of the post-it write WEDNESDAY – Headings you might include are:
- Wednesday share the love.
- Wanting Wednesday.
- Wednesday Wishes.
- Wednesdays Windfalls.

Write 4 post-its with these heading, with a bullet point on what you will talk about that day and place them in a column, next to the TUESDAY post-its.

At the top of the post-it write THURSDAY – Headings you might include are:
- Thankful Thursday.
- Grateful Thursday.
- Thursday Test Pilot.
- Thursday Think Tank.

Write 4 post-its with these heading, with a bullet point on what you will talk about that day and place them in a column, next to the WEDNESDAY post-its.

At the top of the post-it write FRIDAY – Headings you might include are:
- o Friday Wins.
- o Friday Celebrations.
- o Friday Successes.
- o Flipping Friday yay.

Write 4 post-its with these heading, plus a bullet point on what you will talk about that day and place them in a column, next to the THURSDAY post-its.

Okay, by my reckoning, you should now have FOURTEEN columns and 4 rows of post-its. Which means you have 56 days' worth of social media content. Excluding weekends, that's over 2 months' worth of posts, if you are posting every weekday!!!!!! If you decide to only post 3 times a week then you have 4 or 5 months' worth of content! Yes, I know you have got to actually sit and write the posts, but what this exercise does mean is that you do not have to think about what to create, which for me is always the worst bit. Plus, every time you write a post, if you create a social media library then you will soon have a host of posts to choose from.

Now that you have the gist of what to do, look across what lays before you. You can begin to move some of the columns or rows around so that you do not have two posts with the exact same topic next to each other, unless of course that is your intention. You can change some of the comments you made or questions you asked, so it resonates more easily with you. The aim of doing the exercise is to get you started and hopefully you agree that has now been achieved.

Link all of this effort with the fact that on Facebook Pages and Facebook Groups you can schedule content up to two months in advance and you have brought yourself time in your diary to concentrate on other things, whilst being consistent and visible to your Ideal Client. The only commitment now is to make sure you respond each day and that can take up to an hour a day, so schedule it into your standard diary and you are good to go.

If you want to have a look at how this formula works just pop onto my Facebook Group where you will see me putting into action what I teach https://www.facebook.com/groups/StephanieThompsonGetFocusedFastAttractingClients

Another thing about asking "how does social media support your message?" is - the technology takes your message around the globe in minutes. The exposure, once you step out of the shadows, is huge. And that is the best bit of advice I can give you …. "don't be a stalker", actually engage with your Ideal Clients. Allow them to get to "know, like and trust" you. What you have to offer is very much needed, but unless you get visible then clients will not know you are there and how you can help them.

Still stuck on social media content? Here is another option …

Post into your group, or in other groups, asking a relevant question to you, which you can then use the answers to create a plan. You could do a Facebook Poll or just ask a question, which could be something like …… "When posting on Facebook what do you find the most difficult?"

Once you have the responses then group them into headings. Hopefully, you will have 3, 4, 6 or 12 headings depending on the range of answers you received. Within those headings look at your Ideal Clients concerns and jot down all the things that you can share with them that will assist to overcome their problem.

Look at your strategy and how often you are going to post. Draw up a calendar and reflect on the headings as follows:
- o If you have 3 headings, then you have 3 themes per quarter.
- o If you have 4 headings, then you have 4 themes 3 times a year.
- o If you have 6 headings then you have 6 themes twice per year.

Look at the potential resolutions you jotted down in answer to the themes. Start allocating them to the different weeks in the month, days in the week, or months in the year depending on your strategy. This process will at least start your year off and, as necessary, run the poll again with a different question later in the year to develop the rest of your calendar.

It is all about getting them to "know, like and trust" you. By providing a tip on how they can overcome their current situation they will be encouraged to find out what else you have to say next.

I can't emphasise enough …

> **If they know and like you, they will listen,
> it is only once they trust you, will they buy.**

Don't be afraid to use your content again during the year. Your community is continuously changing, plus they may have been on holiday last time and totally missed your post!

And here is one final thing I want to share …

Re-purpose content as often as possible, especially once you know it gains engagement. For example, if you are using video, or podcast, which both have audio then convert it into a written post, which can also become a blog or a newsletter. Add an image for Instagram. Take some soundbites for Twitter. Not everything has to be brand new every day!

As we draw to the end of stage ten, hopefully, you have gained some insight on:
- o The importance of your social media profile.
- o Why it is important to maintain consistent visibility to build that magical "know, like and trust".
- o How to create social media content

I would love to hear about your success, so please do drop me a note to stephanie@stephaniethompsoncoaching.com

Also, if you have any questions, please send them to the same email address above.

Chapter 12 –

How do clients sign up?

Throughout this book I have been sharing all the different steps to help you attract clients and now the time has come for them to sign up. What do you actually need in place to enable that to happen?

Refer back to the big picture you created in Chapter 7. Now you know your content for each stage and have an understanding of social media content and marketing strategy, the next thing is to have a schedule of when you are running your main keynote programme throughout the year. Depending on your beliefs you can align launches with your energy, the moon cycles, pay-days or anything else you want to take into consideration.

Work backwards from each of the dates and put in when you are going to run your low-cost, or free, valuable offer, during which you pitch into your keynote programme. Do make sure you allow time for self-care, because it takes a lot of effort to be present every day in the event answering questions, responding to posts, etcetera.

Working backwards again, when are you going to start marketing your freebie? This is the only time you will do this, because once you start marketing your freebie, it should then become a daily practice.

Wow, now your funnel is planned into the diary and there will be no stopping you!

If you think about the shape of an ordinary kitchen funnel, it gets narrower. This is exactly what will happen with your business funnel.

In fact, draw a funnel and put two lines through it; one about a third of the way down and one about two -thirds of the way down. From the top to the first line write freebie. In the next section write low-cost, or free, valuable offer and in the final narrow bit write programme.

The industry average of sign-ups from the freebie into the programme is 3 to 5%! I am very fortunate, and this is why I teach what I do, because I get a conversion rate of between 10% and 60%. If you want to have a chat about working with me by all means book some time in my diary https://stephanie2.kartra.com/calendar/CoffeeAndChatWithStephanie

Looking at the drawing of the funnel you have just made, I am confident you will now appreciate how many potential clients you want to engage with your freebie to achieve your desired sales. This is why it is important to create a really valuable freebie that clients are anxious to get hold of. It is these people who sign up that are at the start of your funnel.

The freebie is the tempter for your Ideal Client to get to know you more without paying any funds. It is your opportunity to interrupt their current hell and help them want to get to know you more.

By helping these potential clients experience a transformation, for free, they are more likely to want to know what else you can do for them and ultimately you can lead them through to your main programme. All by building that "know, like and trust".

A freebie can take many forms, it is usually a digital document download, but not always, such as
- A check-list
- An e-book
- Ten steps to ......
- 5 tips to ....
- 3 things to avoid when ....
- A planner / layout
- Maybe even a video demonstrating something

A freebie is something that can be downloaded instantly any time of day or night, anywhere in the world. And the key word is instantly.

Imagine this, your potential client has seen one of your posts, they think it will help, so they ask for it. By filling in your opt-in form on the landing page they are asking for your freebie and offering their email address in exchange. Their golden nugget is the document you have created. The email address is the golden nugget for us, as their potential coach.

Once we have their email address then we can nurture them, through our regular newsletters, to take them on a journey, keep them engaged, keep us at the forefront of their mind, build that magical relationship of "know, like and trust". The ultimate aim being to convert them into a paying client.

Struggling to create a freebie? Not sure where to start? Plan beforehand what it is you want to share, with your Ideal Client avatar. Start with the outcome in mind. What is it you want your client to have, feel, experience or gain after following your document? The document often contains simple, straightforward steps or tasks, and will make a big difference to your Ideal Client's current "hell".

Once you know the outcome, you can work on the content. Don't overwhelm them with too much information though. You don't want to put them off before they even start to like you.

Once you know the content, you can work on the most appropriate format to share that content. For example, in a table, bullet points, completed example. Are there any templates you want to include at this point, that your client can download and use?

Now you can work on the words to use, to portray the knowledge you want to impart to your client.

And finally, you can make it look pretty through canva.com or similar.

Now you have a freebie, what's next? The answer is to build a landing page.

A Landing Page is what your client "lands on" to sign up to your freebie. Sometimes it is referred to as an "opt-in page, because your client is "opting in" to your mailing list. Sometimes it is referred to as a sign-up page, or depending on where it is in the funnel, a sales page.

Normally the landing page for a freebie is a very simple document, because your client has already committed to wanting the document through clicking the link they saw. Do promote your freebie, ideally daily, so you can capture the email addresses to build a relationship through your newsletters.

Being consistently visible is the magical ingredient.

A quick recap, so far:
- o You have a freebie and a system to capture the email addresses.

o You have a landing page for the clients to sign up and download your freebie.
o You have outlined your low-cost, or free, valuable offer and your programme, together with the outcomes you are going to deliver
o You have a schedule of events you are going to run, throughout the year, that leads your Ideal Client through your funnel to the point of paying to work with you.

What else do you need?

You may want to create a series of email sequences, scheduled to share early-bird offers, doors closing countdowns, calendar links for discovery calls etc.

I would also like to propose some sort of newsletter, that you send out on a regular basis, sharing what has been happening, what the plans are going forward. Sharing a bit about yourself and maybe sharing a tip or two, so they can make some small transformations. All these topics are to keep them engaged and keep you at the forefront of their mind.

Email sequences and newsletters are shared over several weeks as you gear-up to running your low-cost, or free, valuable offer or free mini masterclass. This is your opportunity to engage with these wonderful souls who are interested in what you are offering. As you near your event, you could engage, in earnest, sharing details about:
o when the event starts
o what will be the benefit of attending the event
o bonuses for early sign-up
o how to book some time to have a chat one-to-one.

It is all part of building the moment and the excitement for their participation.

Recall the funnel we drew earlier in the book? Moving into the low-cost, or free, valuable offer is the middle part of the funnel. Be aware there may be less people in this section than how many signed up for the freebie.

This is very usual behaviour, so don't get disheartened. The more engagement the more chance of conversion, which is the topic of the next Chapter.

Another way to maintain engagement within your low-cost, or free, valuable event is to offer a "hot seat" session, where your audience can book a slot in your calendar to "pick your brains" for free. Many people will snap your hand off to work with you for free.

The thing is; you can have all these wonderful things in place, but if you are not visible and the audience does not know you are there then they will not come.

By being consistently visible in your own and other people's groups they will get to know you.

By being consistent with your branding they will get to identify you, so stop scrolling to see what you have to say.

Every post you put out is a marketing opportunity – I don't mean it has to be a sales pitch with a call-to-action every time. I don't mean it has to be push, push, push. What I do mean is every communication you send out is an opportunity to build connection, to grow that "know, like and trust".

I know I have shared this previously that, due to technology, the attention span is about 8-seconds now. If you have not caught them in those 8-seconds then you have lost the opportunity to engage further. Add on top a potential client sees your message ON AVERAGE, seventeen times before they take action then all I can say is "keep calm and carry on".

Think about your own behaviour whilst on social media. What catches your eye? Why do you stop to look at some and not others?

Think about how many times you have signed up for a freebie yet never looked at it. Have a look in your computer to see how many there are. Every single one of those freebies has valuable information that you wanted at that time for one reason or another.

Think about how many times you have attended the same free or low-cost training. You know the coach is really good. You know the coach will help you in the long run. You know the coach will help you move your business forwards, but there is something holding you back. Yes, it could be funds, but it could be other things too such as time, commitment, being in the right space to accept the training.

In fact, that reminds me of a cartoon I saw many years ago. There was a man, at war, in a full suit of armour with a bow and arrow in his hand fighting the enemy. There was a man stood behind him saying "Excuse me sir, I would like to help you if you would just give me a moment of your time". The first man stays looking straight ahead firing his bow and arrow shouting "Can't you see I am busy? I don't have the time!". Oh, if he had only turned around, just for a second, to see what the second man was offering. For there, behind him, was the answer to everything he was striving to achieve and he could have achieved it in a quarter of the time. Do you want to know what the second man was holding? .... A machine gun and belt of bullets. Had he just turned around for a split second and seen the potential of what was being offered he could have ended the war that day!!!!!!

So my question to you is ...... "what is sitting in your in-box, or your filing system, that actually has the answer to move your business forwards?"

How many challenges have you been in, knowing the coach could actually help you, but you have turned away and continued to do what you have always done?

Remember that old adage ... "If you always do, what you've always done. You'll always get, what you've always got. Perhaps it's time to cast your net on the other side".

I have digressed yet again, so back to where we were ...... you need to be consistently visible for your future Ideal Clients to get to know about you, what you offer, what you can do for them and help them achieve. And that is not achieved by being a stalker!

And here is one final thing I want to share ...

Believe in yourself and your capabilities. Believe in what you can achieve for your clients. Believe the programme you have put together will achieve the outcome your clients desire and deserve. And alongside all of this belief, conquer those self-sabotaging thoughts and have a dream. Know what you are aiming for and celebrate each step as you get closer. Build your confidence in your material and your ability to deliver it confidently and professionally. Adapt and adopt your material as a result of the feedback you receive so you can consistently replicate the outcome for all your clients. And as you grow in confidence, secure in the knowledge you can achieve those transformations, so your fees can grow too.

Oh and here's one final quick tip ...

Know your numbers. Understand, through analysis, how many freebies have been requested compared to how many attended in your low-cost, or free, valuable event, compared to how many signed-up to your programme. Once you know your numbers then you will be able to work out how many freebies need to be shared to achieve the income you desire.

As we draw to the end of stage eleven, hopefully, you have gained some insight on:
- o   The importance of understanding the big picture
- o   What the freebie is trying to achieve and how to develop it.
- o   How having a landing page will capture those magical email addresses.
- o   What an email sequence can achieve as your potential clients move through your funnel.

Remember how you scroll through your phone and what catches your eye? Your potential clients are doing exactly the same thing. Believe in yourself and what you can offer to your clients and to know your numbers.

I would love to hear about your success, so please do drop me a note to stephanie@stephaniethompsoncoaching.com

Also, if you have any questions, please send them to the same email address above.

If you would like any help, please don't hesitate to get in touch
stephanie@stephaniethompsoncoaching.com

Chapter 13 –

Business Mastery

The essence of mastering your business is to offer the X Factor. That "something else" that sets you aside from all the others in your market arena. Often it is a unique combination of training and experience.

What is your x-Factor? What is your unique selling point? What makes you, you?

Combine this with a desire to delight your customer, to exceed their expectations and you are unstoppable.

This is not the only thing you should consider when mastering your business, however it is a key part.

There are three things in business that can hold you paralysed, or even falling backwards.

The first is not staying aware of what is happening, of not keeping up with technology, of not keeping up with your client as they change. It is all about not staying current.

Think about Kodak camera film. Many years ago, Kodak had nearly 70% of the world market for photography. Then cameras went digital before being absorbed into mobile phones. Camera film reels, that you had to take to be developed and then you could view the photos a week later became a thing of the past. As a result, Kodak, one of the most powerful companies in the world folded. The reason? Kodak was so focused on following a winning combination they missed the rise of digital technologies.

Yes, I accept Kodak was a global conglomerate and we are coaches, but think about the fashions in our industry. Perhaps you had never heard of Human Design until only a year ago? Perhaps you had never heard of Keto dieting 5 years ago? Every industry has a fashion cycle and it is good to keep abreast of what is happening. AND then adopt or adapt your approach so you maintain relevance and interest to your ideal client.

You cannot sit back and watch what is happening, you have to evolve personally and also in your business, to be able to keep progressing.

If your business stands still, does not evolve, then in actual fact your business is moving backwards. How so? Because by staying still everyone else is passing you by. Moving with technology can make a real difference here. Look at the introduction of Clubhouse or TikTok just as a brief example!

The second is not following through. Setting goals then not taking action to achieve them. Working with clients and then not staying in touch before, during or after their journey with you. Time waits for no one. If you've planned an event into the diary then make sure you expedite it. Do it now. Prioritise and stick with the plan. Creating a prosperous coaching business comes from taking aligned action.

I am sure you will remember, at the start of the book, I was advocating the need for a compelling big why. The Big Why for why you are in business in the first place. That vision will be achieved only through taking massive aligned action to achieve it. By putting the effort into the hours and making it happen. This is not a "pushing up hill" kind of making it happen, but it does take commitment and dedication to get a business off the ground and maintain momentum of growth, no matter how big or small that business is.

Engage with your tribe and clients, build the interest and then deliver what you promise.

Just because the community is in your Facebook group does not necessarily mean they are engaged. It is up to you to build and maintain their interest. To deliver value. To keep them engaged.

There is nothing worse than being promised the world, so you sign up and then there is no follow-through. How do you know if you have delighted your clients? How do you know if you have delivered what you promised and met their expectations? Are your clients feeling delighted? Are they now your raving fans? Will they spread the word for friends and family to engage with you? You will only find all of this out if you follow up and ask the questions.

PLUS, these are the people, that as you grow and evolve, bring in new programmes and introduce new approaches, will ideally be at the front of the queue waiting to give you money because they know it is going to be good.

And the final one is your own mindset, those mind monkeys, those "fear of ..." or "lack of ...." thoughts and beliefs that go on in your head, or even that you verbalise. If you don't believe in yourself then how can your clients believe in you? Watch your language because like attracts like. If you are sharing negative vibes then more negative vibes will come towards you. How to address your mindset featured in an earlier Chapter.

There are four things a business needs to be able to succeed:

One - Maximise sales – is your funnel fully aligned, in the eyes of the client? Do you have an efficient system that supports your business? Plus, do you have a way of receiving payment from those who want to sign up to your programme? Without clients and sales there is no business so how are you engaging with your clients? Are you stalking in a Facebook group or are you engaging with them? Entering into conversation with them? Providing value so they notice you? Are you building that "know, like and trust" over a period of time? Do you have freebies to share with them to give a taster of what you can achieve for them? All of this counts towards attracting people into your sales funnel, attracting their attention and creating momentum around what you do.

Number Two is the ability to grow your business. Of course, you do not have to grow your business to take over the world, but do ensure your systems allow you the ability to expand, that fits in with your plan and personal goals.

Number Three is the ability to add more and more value for clients, so they keep coming back. They become your raving fans and the best advertising is their "word of mouth" recommendations. Creating raving fans is an essential part of your business hence why it is important to always follow up with your tribe and clients to make sure you have met and, if possible, exceeded their expectations. Word of mouth is really important to attracting more clients. Just to be clear, word of mouth is not only speaking directly to someone at say, a networking event. It is also writing testimonials on your recommendations page, posting how thrilled they were via social media channels, as well as emails received too.

And finally, Number Four is the acknowledgment you are an expert in your field. If you can niche in one area and be known as the expert, your reputation will spread and clients will seek you out.

In addition to the three things that can hold your business paralysed and the four things your business needs to succeed there are also seven things to be able to master your business:

One. Know where you are, realistically (only you need to admit this) and have an effective business plan. You may be applying that old adage "fake it till you make it", which is great for keeping your morale buoyant however if you only have one client then admit, to yourself, you only have one client. Then set a plan for how many clients you want, by when. For example, four new clients by the end of the year. This is quadrupling your business client count, which is a huge step forward! As I said, only you need to know your numbers, but DO be realistic and set realistic goals too.

I am sure you have heard the story about the overnight successful singer who has had 3 number one hits in 3 months. What the headlines don't mention is that individual has probably spent years going round the clubs and pubs finessing their skills, learning all they can about their delivery, how the equipment works, the mechanics inside a recording studio. The 50 Record companies they have approached to publish their material. So don't always believe the headlines and know that success takes commitment and work.

Two. Staying relevant within the industry with a brand that can grow as you grow. Maybe you have reflected on Sir Cliff Richards or Sir Tom Jones, the singers and how they have been in the entertainment business for many decades. Maybe if you are a Kellogs Cornflakes fan, I am sure you will have seen how the packaging has changed over the years, however they are still cornflakes. Whichever example you are thinking about, it has all come about because their brand has grown and evolved by staying relevant within the industry and are in touch with what their fans want. They have kept up with the fashion. Even Coke-Cola with their various adverts.

Another approach is your logo. Will it grow with you as you expand and evolve? If you have looked at my website you will see that I use stars. I love my stars. Stars are virtually ageless. Ok maybe over time the shape of the stars might change, or the colours might change, but the logo will still be stars. My logo can stay relevant as I grow.

Three. Consistent improvement in what you promise to your clients and also how you market it. What worked years ago may not be so successful today. No matter how much your business expands marketing will always be essential, so now is the time to get used to doing it. Think about Vax or Currys or Walmart or Coke-Cola they are all huge companies and yet you will still see regular adverts on the TV for their products. Marketing never ever ends.

Four. Always finess your sales process. Keep the process as simple as possible and use a reliable business system. People have to be able to find you. This does not mean spending thousands on Facebook ads though. It means growing your sales process as you grow. Start off with an organic reach and evolve when you have funds to support. Only spend what you can really afford to lose in case the advert does not get the results you anticipated. And make sure you know your Facebook Insight figures so you know if the adverts are working or not.

Five. Always be aware of your financial and business metrics. Know your Key Performance Indicators. Understand the conversion rates you are able to achieve, so you can plan to achieve your business financial goals.

Six. Regularly update and improve your products or services and the value you provide. This is achieved through remaining up to date with what fashion is occurring in your industry.

Seven. Nurture and create raving fans throughout the year, because they will help you build your business. Remember the story I shared in a previous Chapter, about the big business executives who used word of mouth more than anything else in their business? It is the raving fans that will promote you by word of mouth.

Be aware, budgeting is really helpful, especially when you are first setting up your business and funds are low. Set and stick with the budgets as you do not want to go into debt.

And please, please, PLEASE back up your data regularly be it to a memory stick, the cloud or wherever. Not only are you obliged to do so to meet relevant legislation and regulations you also do not want to lose your business data!

And over-arching everything is having a plan, being organised, using reliable business systems, taking courage and taking action to achieve your dreams.

It's easy when you know how.

If you would like to know how we can work together please contact me at stephanie@stephaniethompsoncoaching.com
I would love to hear from you.

Oh and here's one final quick tip ....
Be your authentic self. In everything you do. Be you. Don't try to be something different because potential clients will see right through it and won't engage with you. Be true to you, walk towards your dreams and celebrate every win, treat yourself every week for a job well done, treat yourself for every milestone achieved. Get those addictive dopamine hits and celebrate your successes.

As we draw to the end of stage twelve, hopefully, you have gained some insight on:
- o The importance of identifying your X-Factor
- o Understanding the three things that can paralyse a business
- o Understanding the four things a business needs to succeed
- o Understanding the seven things needed to be able to master your business.

Unfortunately, it is time for me to go now. Thank you so much for your time. It has been an honour to share my knowledge with you over these Chapters

You can find out more about working me with through
www.stephaniethompsoncoaching.com

Or, if you have any questions, you can email at
stephanie@stephaniethompsoncoaching.com

I look forward to talking with you then.

Take care.

About the author

Stephanie is a multi-award winning, international business empowerment coach, number one international best-selling co-author of "The Untethered Woman", international radio presenter of "Stephanie's Business Coaching Show", global speaker, has appeared on TV and Radio, and founder of the Get Focused Academy.

Learning to be a coach provides a wonderful set of transformational skills. Establishing a business requires a whole different skill set. After being totally overwhelmed by how to start an online coaching business, Stephanie put the knowledge she gained, working around small, medium and global corporate enterprises, together with her own personal holistic journey of self-discovery, into creating an international coaching business for heart-centred coaches and entrepreneurs.

Running 3 successful companies and having helped hundreds of coaches around the globe, Stephanie now focuses her time, through the Get Focused Academy, sharing empowered approaches for coaches to become the star in their own businesses.

Stephanie is THE coach you absolutely have to have if you are ready to expand your online coaching business.

Stephanie can be found at the following links:

Website:
https://www.StephanieThompsonCoaching.com

Facebook:
https://www.facebook.com/groups/StephanieThompsonGetFocusedFastAttractingClients

LinkedIn:
 https://www.linkedin.com/in/stephanie-thompson-937872b/

Resources and references

Yvette Taylor –
Energy Alignment Method (EAM)
www.energyalignmentmethod.com

Thespruce.com, by Anji Cho, to do your Energy number or your Kua number calculation and then there is a link to take you through to determine your success corner direction too.
https://www.thespruce.com/what-is-a-feng-shui-kua-number-1275185

Paul McKenna –
Paul McKenna quotes in his book "Change your life in 7 days" … "The Universe puts one more step in between you thinking of what you want and actually getting it – the action step".

Paul McKenna
Visualisation is a VERY powerful tool. Paul McKenna quotes in his book "Change your life in 7 days" … "For centuries people thought it was impossible to run a four-minute mile. Then on 6 May 1954 Roger Bannister did what all great pioneers do - he made the impossible happen. Within a year of Bannister breaking the four-minute mile, 37 other people around the world had done so as well. In the following year, an incredible 300 runners broke through that previously impenetrable barrier. The finest minds of the age had believed it was impossible to do and their beliefs became a self-fulfilling prophecy. It took one counter-example - one person proving that what they had previously thought could not be done was possible - for everyone else to tap into that possibility within themselves. Bannister was no different to any other runner except for one thing ….. He visualised achieving the goal and he believed he was able to do it.

Don't Quit by Edgar Albert Guest

Andy Harrison –
I saw a quote from Andy Harrington recently. Andy trains in public speaking and crafting your story. The quote said: "If you want to make it big and turn passion into profit, you'll need to create a business that begins by offering an information product that is written, audio and visual format".

Dauchsy Meditations on YouTube

All graphics in this book were created by Stephanie A Thompson in the free version of Canva.com

Printed in Great Britain
by Amazon

82483065R10088